CONSTRUCTING THERAPEUTIC NARRATIVES

CONSTRUCTING THERAPEUTIC NARRATIVES

HAIM OMER AND NAHI ALON

JASON ARONSON INC.
Northvale, New Jersey
London

The authors gratefully acknowledge permission to reprint material from "Collected Poems" by C. P. Cavafy. Copyright © 1975, 1992 revised edn. by Keeley / Sherrard, trans. Reprinted by permission of Princeton University Press.

Director of Editorial Production: Robert D. Hack

This book was set in 12 point Baskerville by TechType of Ramsey, New Jersey, and printed and bound by Book-mart Press of North Bergen, New Jersey.

10 9 8 7 6 5 4 3 2 1

Library of Congress Cataloging-in-Publication Data

Omer, Haim.
Constructing therapeutic narratives / by Haim Omer and Nahi Alon.
p. cm.
Includes bibliographical references and index.
ISBN 1-56821-856-7 (hardcover : alk. paper)
1. Personal construct therapy. 2. Storytelling — Therapeutic use.
3. Constructivism (Psychology) 4. Narration (Rhetoric) 5. Self-perception. 6. Reconstruction (Psychoanalysis) I. Alon, Nahi.
II. Title.
[DNLM: 1. Psychoanalytic Therapy — methods. 2. Psychoanalytic Interpretation. WM 460.6 055c 1996]
RC489.P46044 1996
616.89'14 — dc20
DNLM/DLC
for Library of Congress 96-13384

Printed in the United States of America on acid-free paper. For information and catalog, write to Jason Aronson Inc., 230 Livingston Street, Northvale, New Jersey 07647-1731. Or visit our website: http://www.aronson.com

This book is dedicated to our mothers,
Sonia Kuperman and Mina Alon,
and to the memory of our fathers,
Abraham Kuperman and Gedaliahu Alon.

CONTENTS

INTRODUCTION

Why is narrative crucial to psychotherapy? Because our clients come to us with powerful stories about themselves, characterized by bleak self-portrayals, inexorable plots, narrow themes, and demoralizing meanings. How can we compete with such stories that are not only well-rehearsed but also backed by mountains of selective negative evidence—stories so persuasive that the client does not view them as stories at all, but as slices of life? We must build, together with the client, stories that are no less compelling. We must pitch portrayal against portrayal, plot against plot, theme against theme, and meaning against meaning. It will not do, however, simply to write a new story in opposition to the old one. To succeed, the new story must be close enough to the client's experience so that she[1] may view it as *her* story; on the other hand, it must be different enough from the old story, so as to allow for new meanings and options to be perceived.

In the past, therapists believed that only the client dealt in stories while psychotherapy offered truth. We felt safely grounded on the objectivity of science. Gradually, however, doubts as to the extent of this grounding started to creep in. In the process of learning to doubt, we have also, at times, understood that the mantle of science was not only protective but also cumbrous. We are still puzzling about this issue and our precise relationship with scientific knowledge and method is far from resolved. Still, we have gone far enough to know that an important part is played in psychotherapy by elements that resist a scientific approach. This is the realm of narrative.

Narrative entered psychotherapy as a counterpoise to the objective, the factual, the unalterably given. One of the earliest expressions of this new perspective, Spence's *Narrative Truth and Historical Truth* (1982), is an extended argument against the very possibility of neutral or objective data in psychoanalysis. The Freudian belief that the truth of psychoanalytic reconstruction is logically compelling is rejected by Spence in favor of the legitimacy and importance of *narrative truth*: all we can aspire to is a coherent, satisfying, and pragmatically valuable account of the client's life, which may gainfully replace the previous self-defeating one. We want to be able to answer like Picasso, when

1. Throughout the book we alternate feminine and masculine pronouns.

told that his portrait of Gertrude Stein did not resemble her: "Don't worry. It will."

The idea of narrative truth spread across the various schools of psychotherapy, quickly assuming avalanche proportions. Within psychoanalysis, Spence's book was echoed and abetted by Schafer's *The Analytic Attitude* (1983). For Schafer, even the ideal of *one* coherent narrative is unattainable: all we can ever achieve is an everchanging sheaf of interconnected retellings, each reflecting the therapeutic relationship at the moment in which it occurred.

Independently of these developments within psychoanalysis, the field of family and strategic therapy also embraced the narrative idea: Watzlawick's book *The Invented Reality* (1984) is a collection of old and new articles by many authors who favor the view that reality is constructed rather than discovered. This new approach, which became known as *constructivism*, was to have a decisive influence on the field, becoming the banner of two opposing camps: (1.) those who claimed that since historical truth had been debunked, therapists were now free to concoct narratives at their own discretion and sell them to clients; and (2.) those who claimed that with the demise of presumed objectivity therapists had lost all claim to privileged knowledge and should therefore approach their clients in a humble attitude of *not-knowing*: all hierarchy and directiveness were but a hollow show (Anderson and Goolishian 1988, Hoffman 1985, 1988, 1992). The eternal issue of *manipulation* underlies this debate.

The narrative idea has made converts even within the very ramparts of psychotherapeutic positivism.

Cognitive therapists (Russell 1991, Russell and Van den Broek 1992), for instance, have tried to pinpoint the conditions that enable a new narrative to supplant the old one. In their view the process is similar to one that occurs when one scientific theory replaces another: the new theory has to account not only for the evidence, but also for the successes of the old one. Thus, Einstein's theory supplanted Newton's, not only because of its predictive power but also because it explained the success of the Newtonian approach. Similarly in psychotherapy, a new narrative would best succeed if it could explain how the old one came to be embraced.

The narrative approach has proved fertile also in practice. Within the psychoanalytic tradition, Strupp and Binder (1984) proposed a brand of short-term therapy based on the narrative structure of personal episodes: clients in their view, lost a sense of control over their lives because their self-narratives were punctured by lacks and leaps. Therapy should help them improve their ability in self-narration by pointing out which structural narrative links they consistently missed. Therapy thus became an applied course in story-grammar.

Another approach was pursued by strategically minded therapists who developed what came to be known as *solution–orientation* (de Shazer 1985, O'Hanlon and Weiner-Davis 1989). These authors helped their clients reconstruct life episodes around solutions, rather than problems. A problem focus, they argued, leads to problem-saturated narratives which blind the protagonist to possible options; a solution focus, on the other hand, creates a positive selective blindness to problems, ridding the way of potential obstacles.

Perhaps the most influential of all practical narrative approaches is the one put forth in White and Epston's (1990) *Narrative Means to Therapeutic Ends*. This approach to narrative reconstruction is based on a double characterization: (1.) the client's problem is personalized and externalized as an agency bent on subjugating him, and (2.) the client is redescribed as the person he could become, once freed from the problem's yoke. Therapy is the client's war of liberation from the problem's degrading domination.[2]

Once we define psychotherapy as a discipline that deals with narratives, it is only natural that we should ask ourselves what we can learn from other disciplines that had already perfected this medium for hundreds of years. In this book, as we develop our therapeutic principles of narrative reconstruction, we shall draw from the potential similaritites between psychotherapy and the lettered professions, searching by their light how to do better what we do in any case: characterize, construct plot, outline and develop themes, and convey meanings.

Chapter 1—*Narrative Empathy and Therapeutic Splitting*, presents the book's major tools of narrative reconstruction. By means of these two ideas, we shall try to

2. These examples do not, of course, exhaust the treatment approaches that could qualify as narrative. Polster's (1987) contribution to humanist psychotherapy, the Milan School's approach to family therapy (Boscolo et al. 1987), the work of the Galveston group (Anderson and Goolishian 1988), and the use of *the reflecting team* (Andersen 1987) are a few additional notable examples.

steer our course through the thorny issues of client-authorship versus therapist-authorship, therapeutic support versus confrontation, and problem versus solution orientation.

Chapter 2—*Characters,* illustrates how a narrative, rather than psychopathological approach to characterization, can broaden our perspective and enrich our dialogue with clients. We present clinical illustrations of three character types and the particular conversational styles that may be appropriate to them: the romantic, the picaresque, and the epic.

Chapter 3—*Plots,* deals with the development of narrative lines. A variety of devices for maintaining involvement, curiosity, and momentum to keep the plot going, are discussed and illustrated.

Chapter 4—*Themes,* deals with the formulation and elaboration of therapeutic themes as manifested in the vicissitudes of thematic unity, recapitulation, variation, and alternation.

Chapter 5—*Meanings,* is an attempt to pull together the strands of the previous chapters so as to answer the question: "What makes for a meaningful therapeutic narrative?" This chapter offers guidelines for the development of a narrative of which the client may say: (1) "This is my story"; (2) "I am the hero of this story"; (3) "This story has a future."

Chapter 6—*A Narrative Attitude to Psychotherapy,* summarizes the therapist's narrative angle as described in this book.

In Chapter 7—*Historical Foundations of the Narrative Approach,* we present our view of the theoretical developments that ushered in the narrative perspective in psychotherapy. We review the work of thinkers such as Erving Goffman, Ronald Laing, Thomas Szasz, Michel Foucault, Gregory Bateson, Elizabeth Loftus, Donald Spence, Roy Schafer, Jerome Bruner, and Kenneth Gergen, who, to our mind, contributed the most to the decline of the positivist and realist approach to psychotherapy. This theoretical chapter might be viewed as an appendix. We feel, however, that it supplies the intellectual justification for our whole enterprise.

One word of explanation and perhaps of apology: although psychotherapeutic narratives are a joint work, this book focuses on the craftsmanship of the therapist. It is not our intention, however, to imply that all the art comes from the therapist and all the mess from the client: the therapist's major skill is precisely to match the client's experience and be guided by her voice. Thus, although we shall be talking about the therapist's art of characterization, plot construction, thematic elaboration, and conveyance of meaning, we shall see that in these very activities we act most therapeutically when we most allow ourselves to be led by our clients, our partners.

psychotherapy, we present the work of theorists such as Irving [illegible], Ronald Laing, [illegible] Mitchell, [illegible] Gregory Bateson, [illegible] Donald Spence, Roy Schafer, [illegible] and [illegible], who [illegible] more to the dangers of the positivist and realist approach to psychotherapy. This introductory chapter might be viewed as [illegible] however, [illegible] the [illegible] purposes.

One word of explanation and [illegible] although [illegible] is not our intention, however, to [illegible] from the therapist [illegible] the client's [illegible] and be [illegible] This [illegible] should be [illegible] of characterization, [illegible] and [illegible] we [illegible] which we must allow ourselves to [illegible].

1

NARRATIVE EMPATHY AND THERAPEUTIC SPLITTING

The major question in all discussions about therapeutic narratives seems invariably to be: Whose story is it? One side argues that only the client's own, self-authored story can ever be therapeutic; that the process of therapy is precisely one of helping the client become liberated from all external impositions or additions; and that influence is the demon that tempts therapists to betray their mission and robs clients of the ownership of their lives. The other side in the debate argues that we (therapists or anyone else) cannot *not* influence, just as we cannot *not* communicate; that silence, acceptance, confirmation, and questioning are also forms of influence; and that the presumption not to influence is tantamount to the unwitting exertion of influence. In this book, we want to take the dilemma by both horns: in influencing our clients' construction of personal narratives, our task is precisely to search for a form of persuasion that participates most profoundly in the client's truth. Indeed, we must influence, but our influence will only be therapeutic if we learn to mold it to the client's experience. This process demands from therapists not only a continuous vigilance regarding our own views, values, and descriptions, but also a constant effort at self-transcendence. We are, thus, very active narrators but we narrate most therapeutically when we are most guided by our client's promptings. In this chapter we will define our two major tools for furthering this client-guided therapeutic influence: *narrative empathy* and *therapeutic splitting*. The first embodies our attempt to fit the therapeutic narrative to the contours of the client's experience; the second, the attempt to narrate therapeutically not only what is good and positive about the client's patterns, but also what is bad and damaging.

NARRATIVE EMPATHY

Consider the following interchange:

> A 35-year old widow asked one of us for help with what she described as "AIDS panic." Half a year before, after a night in which she had taken LSD for the first time in her life, she woke up with the inner certainty that a man she had had sex with a few days before had infected her with AIDS. Repeated negative tests in the following months failed to allay her constant anxiety. She was also plagued by fears that she was going crazy. She stopped socializing, her involvement with work

decreased, she slept badly and, worst of all, to her mind, she started to neglect her children.

Although this had been her first experience with LSD, she had used marijuana for quite a while. A few years before, after the death of her husband, she would sometimes smoke a joint to help her support her grief. She would also indulge in sex for the same purpose: the flirting and the sexual pleasure made her forget her pain for a while. Gradually, she began smoking daily, even many times in a single day. Casual sex also became a fixture of her life. She could not think of a weekend when she had not gone to bed with a man. Only upon inquiry, did she tell me[1] that she felt very bad about these activities. She called herself a "junky" and a "light woman" and feared that the children would be hurt, but she could not bring herself to stop. Both activities, however, had almost disappeared in the last few months. Sex had become aversive to her because of the anxiety it aroused and marijuana as well, because of the fear that she was crossing the border to heavier drugs. The anxiety, however, was making her life unbearable.

I told her that, apart from her fears, she seemed depressed. The depression might have to do not only with the fears but also with the fact that since the death of her husband it was the first time she was living with her grief without the consolation of sex or marijuana. As for her fears, I told her that though she had neither AIDS nor any mental illness, the anxiety seemed to make very good sense. It was an alarm reaction, a powerful ringing of bells, warning her that she was in great danger. She knew all along that her involvement

---

1. Throughout the book, we change into the first person singular when we describe cases that were treated or supervised by one of us.

> with drugs and sex were leading her into a blind alley. By her own standards she was becoming addicted and promiscuous. Her dependence had grown and all her resolutions had turned into smoke. After she took the LSD, the alarm sounded with all its might. It was effective. She stopped the two behaviors that were endangering her. Why then, did the alarm not stop as well? Probably because she was not sure of herself. She still smoked an occasional joint and still went to bed at times with casual acquaintances. Probably she was still afraid, and with good reason, that without the panic she would slip again. To go on panicking was for the moment her only assurance against danger. To overcome the problem she would have to hold a serious dialogue with her alarm system. She would have to acknowledge its services and convince it that she was trustworthy. She said this description answered exactly to what she had been feeling.

This process of developing a therapeutic narrative that discloses the inner logic of the client's seemingly irrational behavior is what we term *narrative empathy*. Let us explain.

In his narrative interpretation of psychoanalysis, Roy Schafer (1983) proposed a new view of the process of empathy. Traditionally, therapeutic empathy was conceived as an emotional echo: the therapist reverberated with the client's feelings and the communication of this experience helped the client feel accepted and understood. This kind of response certainly plays a role not only in psychotherapy but in all positive forms of interaction: people use their inner emotional echoes to understand others and to make others feel understood.

Schafer argues, however, that in psychotherapy this is often not enough. In empathizing directly with the client's pain, the therapist may be providing the client with a rather common experience, for the expression of suffering often awakens sympathy. What is for Schafer more pertinent to psychotherapy is for the therapist to empathize not only with the client's expressed suffering but with the feelings underlying his problematic or even obstreperous behavior. This is, of course, more rare: people do not naturally empathize with someone who steps on their toes. But, are therapists supposed to be saints? Not so, says Schafer. We can empathize with the client's problematic patterns, not by any spontaneous and immediate emotional response, but by a process of construal: we assume that developing the problem behavior was the client's best possible way of surviving under the conditions in which he grew. We thus empathize, not with the obstreperous client as such, but with the one whose story we construe.

Empathic Narrative vs External Narrative

An empathic narrative can best be understood if it is contrasted to an external one in which the protagonist is described, as it were, from the outside. The key to an empathic narrative is participation; the key to an external one is detachment. In an empathic narrative the inner logic of the protagonist's behavior stands revealed, so that one might say that in similar circumstances one might behave likewise; in an external one, the protagonist is depicted as basically different from us. Psychotherapists make use of both kinds of narratives. Thus, when we describe a client's behavior in diagnostic terms as the result of blind conflictual forces, or of reinforcement contingencies, our narratives are external. We may need those descriptions to make theoretical sense of the material, to communicate with other professionals, or to make administrative decisions. We should not assume, however, that clients can accept them at face value, for they cannot recognize themselves in such terms (even if they seem to in order to please the therapist). The seal of an empathic description, on the other hand, is precisely that it allows for self-recognition. When faced with it, the client can say: "That's me!" In fact, what is often viewed as resistance may be the result of our assuming that the client must accept an external narrative as if it were an empathic one.

The empathic narrative in therapy does not arise fullblown: we characterize, narrate, and empathize piecemeal, with each step guiding the other. Thus, in meeting a client for the first time, we can only develop a hypothesis, a tentative description, a rudimentary sketch of character. In this we are drawn to empathize, for we can only characterize by speculating how it feels to be such a person.[2] Gradually through this empathic guessing, we expand on our initial sketch and eventually outgrow it. Indeed, if we are endowed even with minimal capacity for narrative empathy, our initial narratives and character molds will usually prove too

2. Even a caricature involves a measure of identification, as when the person who does the caricature imitates by posture, facial expression, or tone of voice, the characteristics of the caricatured object.

narrow for the feelings we experience in trying to penetrate them. The process of developing a therapeutically empathic narrative involves, thus, a constant effort at self-transcendence: it is by casting off our limited descriptions that we can best help the client overcome her own.

A constant tension between an external narrative and an evolving empathic one is manifest in Shakespeare's characterization of Shylock, in *The Merchant of Venice*. The play's ideology is obviously anti-Jewish. Christian mercy is set against Jewish legalism; Christian generosity against Jewish greed; Christian love against Jewish revenge. Shylock's downfall, his daughter's elopement, and his forced conversion were probably experienced by the play's audiences as more than justified: they are no more than the just payment for Shylock's moral turpitude. In the *DSM-IV* of Shakespeare's era, Shylock would figure as a perfect illustration of the spiritual pathology of being a Jew. We are clearly within the boundaries of external narrative.

However, in attempting to come closer to Shylock's character so as to portray him vividly on the stage, Shakespeare overstepped the boundaries of his own external description and was lured by his own creative empathy to portray Shylock's behavior as evolving logically from his condition. So much so, that Shylock's vengeful outbursts become almost the only plausible thing to do. Empathy and characterization come closest together in what is probably Shylock's best-known speech:

Salerio: Why, I am sure if he forfeit thou wilt not take his flesh. What's that good for?

Shylock: To bait fish withal. If it will feed nothing else, it will feed my revenge. He hath disgraced me, and hindered me half a million, laughed at my losses, my bargains, cooled my friends, heated mine enemies and what's his reason? I am a Jew. Hath not a Jew eyes? Hath not a Jew hands, organs, dimensions, senses, affections, passions?—fed with the same food, hurt with the same weapons, subject to the same diseases, healed by the same means, warmed and cooled by the same winter and summer as a Christian is? If you prick us, do we not bleed? If you tickle us, do we not laugh? If you poison us, do we not die? And if you wrong us, shall we not revenge? If we are like you in the rest, we will resemble you in that. If a Jew wrong a Christian, what is his humility? Revenge! If a Christian wrong a Jew, what should his sufferance be by Christian example? Why revenge! The villainy you teach me I will execute, and it shall go hard but I will better the instruction.

(*The Merchant of Venice, III.i.*)

Revenge thus becomes empathically transparent. However different our own preferences may be, Shylock's begin to be emotionally acceptable. Through narrative empathy, his Jewish symptoms have found a human habitation in which we can momentarily feel at home. Shakespeare does not stop at that, however: the work of empathy pursues its course *in defiance* of the external stereotype, outgrowing it and almost casting it off as a dry husk. Shylock's conversation with Tubal, after the elopement of his daughter Jessica with a quantity of his gold and jewels begins quite stereotypically:

Tubal: Your daughter spent in Genoa, as I heard, one night fourscore ducats.

Shylock: Thou stick'st a dagger in me. I shall never see my gold again. Fourscore ducats at a sitting, fourscore ducats.

Tubal: There came divers of Antonio's creditors in my company to Venice that swear he cannot choose but break.

Shylock: I am very glad of it. I'll plague him; I'll torture him. I am glad of it.

Tubal: One of them showed me a ring that he had of your daughter for a monkey.

Shylock: Out upon her! Thou torturest me, Tubal. It was my turquoise; I had it of Leah when I was a bachelor. I would not have given it for a wilderness of monkeys.

(*The Merchant of Venice, III.i.*)

So Shylock does care infinitely more for the human than for the material value of the ring! The person has outgrown the persona. Thus is our view of character changed through narrative empathy. In the play, the tension is never resolved: Shakespeare alternates between an empathic and an external view of Shylock. In psychotherapy we hope that as treatment proceeds we may become more and more able to shed the external in favor of the empathic narrative.

Beware! Beware!

John came to treatment complaining of extreme anxiety regarding medical treatments. Many years before, three weeks after receiving his driver's license, he had been tempted to show off his driving prowess to a girl. Lacking the skill to match his daring, he smashed his car against a wall, the tank caught fire, and he suffered severe burns and injuries to his legs, one of which had to be amputated. Miraculously the girl came out unscathed. Now, at the age of 40, he had to undergo a series of medical tests and treatments that he kept postponing on account of his fears. Most of all, the very thought of anesthesia and hospitalization paralyzed him. He asked the therapist, skeptically, whether she could help him. He also inquired in detail about her professional approach: he had studied social work and was well-informed about the different styles and approaches to therapy. When the therapist commented that John seemed uncertain about commiting himself to the therapy, John said he was planning to interview several therapists so as to decide which one suited him best. He said that in the past he had had two negative treatment experiences that had made him wary. However, he had also had one good therapy experience, that unfortunately he had been forced to interrupt because he moved to another city.

As a child, he remembered himself as active, open, and sociable. In adolescence, however, he became gradually lonely and suspicious. He also felt cut off from his parents whom he described as incapable of any contact except of an offensive nature. Gradually his isolation deepened. Ironically, his accident occurred precisely when he was trying for once to break out of it.

John described his life during the first few months after the accident as completely dominated by the pain. His only thought and wish was for the pain to be taken away. The daily treatments were harrowing. He felt that the doctors and nurses mishandled him, exchanging his bandages with no consideration for his agonizing pain. There was only one young nurse who knew how to change his bandages slowly and carefully, causing him almost no pain. Unfortunately she did it only rarely,for she worked in his ward as part of a course only one day a week. One recurrent frustrating experience of his hospital stay were his mother's daily visits. She would sit by him crying all the time. Her crying depressed him and he hated her for it. He disliked it even more when she touched him. He told enviously of another young man with severe back injury whose mother supported him fully throughout his convalescence, becoming to John's mind, his very backbone. The therapist commented that John seemed torn between his longing for support and his fear of closeness. She later used this story of the two different mothers as a metaphor for his main problem in life and in therapy.

At the very beginning of his hospital stay, the ward psychologist had asked whether he had related his traumatic experience to the therapy group and whether he had cried over the loss of his leg. He said he had told the story but had not cried. She ventured that he would surely cry in the coming session. He did not. He felt, however, that something had gone wrong because he had failed to cry. He envied another young man in the therapy group who told the story of his own accident amid a flood of tears. John wished he had been capable of such a degree of emotional release. Even now, more than twenty years after the event, he believed that if he could only achieve a vivid recall of the trauma and give full vent to his suppressed feelings, his anxiety and depression would clear up. He added that in his one good experience with therapy in the past, he felt he had come closer to this needed catharsis.

It took John a full year to adapt to the prosthesis. Gradually, however, he became more active and joined a sports team for the handicapped. He started to date but, as he angrily told the therapist, women almost never understood him. The one exception, a woman friend he had been dating for almost two years, failed in another respect: she did not attract him sexually. John was also highly critical of the therapist, especially her behavior at the beginning of the sessions. He implied that if she were more sensitive she would know what he needed and how to address him as each session started. As the therapist saw it, John expected to be met on his own terms without having to go through the trouble of saying what they were! She felt that this rigid expectancy and the anger that invariably followed its frustration pointed to John's deepseated difficulty with intimacy.

After John had adapted to the prosthesis, his life for a while seemed to be opening up. He traveled a lot and studied social work. Once more, however, he had to be hospitalized because of an infectious disease. This renewed contact with illness and hospitalization proved a negative turning point. He developed acute anxiety and endless bodily complaints that he believed to be psychosomatic. He also suffered from renewed pains in his stump due to a known problem that would respond to minor surgery but which he failed to undergo because of his fear of medical treatment. He also had paralyzing cardiac fears. Gradually he stopped swimming and exercising and was all but confined to his home by pain and anxiety.

After finishing his studies John began an internship in family therapy but cut it short, feeling he could not treat others before he treated himself. He decided instead to study philosophy. All of his choices, including this one, seemed to be pointing in the direction of a lessening involvement with actual life. In therapy, too, all interpersonal issues had to be postponed until the anxiety and the psychosomatic complaints had been resolved. John expected this to occur at one stroke, for instance, by a big abreactive bang that would release him from the trauma. However, when the therapist asked John to describe the accident in detail, he replied that it was no use: all he could recall were dry memories, empty of feeling, that he had already related many times before. The therapist felt that the pains, the anxiety, and the trauma were John's way of absenting himself from life. They were also his way of paralyzing the therapy.

In her attempt to release the therapy from its barren involvement with John's complaints about pain and anxiety, the therapist raised the possibility of medication. John felt the therapist was dumping him on the psychiatrist out of despair. He needed a strong therapist who was sure of her way and what he was getting instead was a shillyshallying, despondent one! He even thought of traveling to his previous therapist's hometown to ask her opinion about his current therapy.

When this crisis cooled, John told the therapist that he had started to attend a bioenergy group. She encouraged him, saying that the bioenergy might be a good outlet for his anxiety and perhaps help him with the pain. The therapist might then become freer to deal with John's relational problems. Again, John felt rejected and suggested she was giving up on him. All attempts of the therapist to focus on John's defensive behavior, his avoidance of commitment, and his fear of contact and intimacy aroused similar responses. John would go back to his anxiety and pain and complain that the therapist was giving up without actually saying so. After three very frustrating months of therapy, the therapist brought the case to a group consultation conducted by one of the authors.

Initially, the group discussion focused on possible ways of understanding and overcoming John's defensiveness. The group, however, was quite pessimistic, feeling that John's attachment to physical complaints seemed to have turned into his character armor. Such a critical and pessimistic attitude towards the client's rigidness is a sure sign of an external narrative. Indeed, it is the rare client who can recognize himself in such a description. Could we renarrate John's behavior in acceptable terms? What follows is the message we elaborated in the consultation.

"I have been thinking about your feeling that I do not really understand you. In some major respect, I think that you were right. I had failed to perceive the inner logic of your behavior. I had implied that your anxiety and sometimes even your pain were actually defenses against intimate relating. I would now like to correct this biased perspective.

"My new understanding began with the trauma. You felt all along that the trauma had not been adequately expressed, understood, and dealt with. You hoped that if you could, once and for all, give full expression to the traumatic experience, things would start to change. I was puzzled about this and even asked for a professional consultation on the matter. I came to realize that over and beyond the accident itself you were badly and continuously traumatized throughout your hospitalization. For months on end, your continuous experience was: I am in pain! Treatment is bad and causes more pain! I will have no control! These thoughts, sensations, and feelings filled your whole mind, leaving no space for other matters. Excruciating pain and the certain fear of even more excruciating pain drove out all other interests; treatment was almost invariably hurtful and inconsiderate, and control was a rare experience belied by your forced passivity and the unbearable sensations with which you were continuously bombarded. Moreover, your mother's visits, the only regular contact you had, were a caricature of human closeness: she demoralized you and you feared her very touch. This traumatization went on and on, giving rise to an overruling need to preserve and protect yourself. Since you came out of the hospital, you seem to be saying all the time: Beware! Beware! You feel you cannot trust your body not to betray you. You feel you cannot lose control. You feel you cannot trust potential treators, even if apparently well-intentioned. Your wariness towards me and others becomes justified as does your need to know what is going on all the time. And so does your unwillingness to put yourself into the hands of doctors and hospitals.

"This continuous traumatization does not, I think, lend itself to one big abreactive experience. We must, like the young nurse who knew how to change your bandages, work with care, checking each of your daily experiences for the underlying pain, respecting your fears and slowing down when you say it hurts. Indeed, this trauma was one of the great formative experiences in your life. Although you were already a somewhat wary and withdrawn person before it, the trauma vastly deepened and generalized these attitudes, transforming them almost into a fear of life. I failed to recognize the legitimate source of your fear. I hope that now as I acknowledge its source, I will be able to disappoint you less. Maybe now I can become a better partner to help you face your present life-challenge: the need to learn once again how to take risks.

"You may find it paradoxical when I say: I understand why you cannot trust me and even so I ask you to trust me. Still, this is precisely the paradox that you face in all areas. Life seems to be saying: Living is unbearable but even so you must live on. Your body seems to be saying: You cannot trust me but even so you must rely on me. Your very common-sense seems to be saying: Risk-taking is absurd but even so you must learn to take risks. I hope, however, that my understanding will make a difference, for I shall no longer imply that you are acting irrationally. With every new challenge, we shall look squarely at the inner logic of its refusal, but also at the opportunity of its acceptance."

This empathic narrative allowed for a better therapeutic dialogue. In describing the message's impact, the therapist referred first of all to herself. She said that the message made her hopeful and acceptant, an attitude that helped her weather the recurrent storms in the therapeutic relationship. Although the therapy remained knotty and John still blamed the therapist for not being sensitive and understanding enough, the dialogue changed. John's focus on his physical complaints all but disappeared from the discussion. The therapy became centered instead on the interpersonal aspects of risk-taking. After a while he resumed his internship in family-therapy and at the end of the year was working in the field. John reframed his chief problem as having to do with his narrow capacity for emotional expressiveness. With this new definition in mind, he decided to stop the therapy (after about a year) and join a group using expressive bodily therapy instead. Four months later, however, he was back. The woman he had been dating for three years and with whom he had a very close friendship had developed terminal cancer. John was badly shaken and asked the therapist to help him deal with this situation which, to his mind, made all his physical complaints seem small. He added that the therapist was the only person who had really understood what he had gone through.

THERAPEUTIC SPLITTING

Consider the following therapeutic transition:

A 17-year-old girl from a very religious Jewish family was brought to therapy because she had disappeared from a school party in the company of a young man. It was the third time such an event, highly unusual in the girl's religious ambiance, had occurred. There was special reason for worry because the girl's mother suffered from manic-depressive illness and had been promiscuous in her manic phases. In the past, the girl had fallen in love quite a few times, each time with the greatest intensity. She also wrote poetry and had already earned a prize in a reputable competition.

The therapist was afraid that the girl was losing control over her impulses and might become promiscuous. She was also worried that the girl might also be showing signs of incipient mania. She tried to help her monitor her feelings and consider the consequences of her acts. This approach led to an impasse. The girl left therapy and it was only with great difficulty that she was persuaded to come again.

A group consultation helped develop a new therapeutic narrative and attitude. The therapist must acknowledge the central role that fiery feelings played in the girl's life: she needed them as a person and as a writer. To suppress these feelings was, for her, to betray her very self. The big question, however, was whether they would warm or burn her—whether she would end up with a rich or a devastated life. Love might sensitize her as a person and a poet, but might also render her pregnant or promiscuous. The therapist was sure that the girl's life would be stormier than that of most other young women of her social set. Indeed, her romanticism

> was not one of genteel niceties but of a rougher kind. The therapist was less frightened now that she understood. Yet, she believed the girl would be playing false to her own feelings if she allowed them to vulgarize or debase her. This new narrative allowed for a steady therapeutic dialogue that was also more open and rich than the previous one.[3]

This dual unfolding of the positive and negative sides of the problem in a unified therapeutic story is what we call *therapeutic splitting*. A recurrent issue in modern therapeutic debate is whether treatment should focus on the negative or the positive, on problems or solutions, on the pain or the prize. The therapeutic narratives that characterize the leading therapeutic approaches could be easily placed in their relation to these two poles. Thus, toward the bright pole, we might locate behavior therapy and the solution oriented approaches; on the dark one, psychoanalysis and the starker varieties of existential therapy. Schafer (1976) characterized one side as predominately *comic* and the other as *tragic*. In this respect, also, we advocate a synthesis of the extremes: the richer therapeutic narrative is the one that embraces both the positive and the negative, allowing each its due salience and proper role. It is not a lukewarm compromise that we are proposing, but the full expression of both sides.

Therapists of most persuasions agree that clients often pay a heavy price for their one-sided attitudes. Thus, regarding themselves or others as wholly good or bad, viewing a piece of behavior as absolutely laudable

3. A more detailed version of this case appears in Omer (1995).

or objectionable, looking at their past or future as black or white, these totalist positions often spell trouble. *Therapeutic splitting* refers to a therapeutic communication that aims at introducing a double description where a singleminded one has been the rule. The therapist proceeds by splitting the univocal attitude into two contrasting aspects but in such a manner that both can be entertained together. The aim of the intervention is to make room for a more complex narrative and for options that would have been banned out of existence by the more simplistic frame of mind.

Therapeutic splitting is the mirror image of *pathological splitting*. In pathological splitting, the subject, unable to relate to an object as both good and bad, breaks it into two opposite ones. Thus, the human mother with her virtues and failings is split into a wholly good and a wholly bad mother (which, of course, appear at different times). Similarly, the therapist is sometimes viewed as the epitome of all virtues and, at other times, as the sum of all vices. The self is also subjected to this disjunctive process: it is now beauteous, strong, and true; now, ugly, base, and false. Often, one side of the split object all but disappears: thus, the client may meet only with the bad mother, the evil therapist, and the black self (their positive counterparts ruling unopposed in the realm of wishful fantasy). Therapeutic splitting works in the opposite way: faced with a client who expresses a strictly one sided attitude, the therapist brings the two putative sides to mind. However, therapeutic splitting involves more than merely pointing out to the client that there is another side to the coin: the therapeutic message must be so construed that the client will find it hard to entertain one perspective without its counterpart. How is this achieved?

The key is narrative empathy. Both sides of the split must be so narrated that the client can say, "That's me!" Indeed, it is crucial that the negative side of the split be connected to the client's own values and experience. The price and the damage must appear as such in the client's eyes. The same effort must be invested on the positive side. It is useless, for instance, to describe the positive side of a problematic pattern as involving gains that the client cannot actually recognize as such. For instance, telling a family that their symptomatic child sacrifices herself for the good of the family may be no more than an external narrative with which not only the family, but also the therapist, often fail to identify themselves. When, on the contrary, the positive side of the split depicts convincingly to the client the inner logic of her behavior, and the negative side expresses empathically the waste and damage to her life, then we may reasonably expect the client to accept the full description. Rejecting either of the two sides would almost imply the rejection of the other.

Therapeutic splitting is called for whenever the therapist faces a monolithic attitude that seems to block progress. On such occasions, the therapist often feels tempted to react by offering to the client the counterpart of this single-minded attitude. For instance, a self-rejecting client may be met by a supportive therapist; a self-complacent client, by a confrontative therapist. Therapeutic experience shows that these well-intentioned positions often miss the mark. They fail to take hold because they contradict the rule of participation, by clashing too glaringly with the client's immediate experience. Actually, they oppose the client's one-sided attitude by another equally one-sided attitude. Evolving an appropriate therapeutic split may thus be a corrective not only to the client but to the therapist, as well. Furthermore, the split obviates the dichotomy between a supportive and a confrontative therapeutic stance, making them mutually enhancing rather than contradictory. Thus, the client will tend less to discount the therapist's positive appreciation on the grounds that she sees only what is good, or to water down the painful side of the message on the grounds that the therapist sees only what is bad. Likewise, the therapist may allow herself to speak on each side with a fuller voice, knowing that the other side is being given equivalent power.

Cynicism

> Kate was 22 and had no will to live. She would not commit suicide, however, for she felt she had no strength for that, either. In spite of her severe asthma she refused to comply with preventive medical treatment. Consequently she had been recurrently hospitalized with asthmatic attacks and her lung capacity was extremely small. When asked why she did not take her medication so as to breathe better, she answered that she saw no reason to inhale deeply, and that a quarter of a lung was quite enough for the amount of air she desired. She stayed in bed daily till noon, went out for a short while to meet with friends, and returned to bed. She hardly had the energy to make herself a cup of coffee.
>
> The only thing she respected in herself was her intelligence. Most people were stupid and she hardly

ever found someone worth talking to. She saw no future for herself; she did not think she would ever work—maybe study. It might suit her to be a professor at the Hebrew University and be married to some bearded intellectual. She liked children but she did not think she would have any. After talking like this for a while, she would add, with a wave of the hand: "Silly, what I have been saying. I don't really mean what I say. There is nothing behind my words." Sometimes she would cry and this was the only reaction that, for a moment, would pierce her dismissive, cynical mask.

She had recently finished her army service where she had served as a secretary. She despised herself for having taken such a stupid job. Actually, it was agreed in her unit that she could do as she wanted. They were pleased with her because she made them laugh with her sardonic humor. The same had happened in high school. Her teachers had enjoyed her wit so much that they had been willing to put up with her almost total neglect of scholastic work. She felt, however, that it was somebody else who was laughing and making others laugh. Her real self lived inside a bubble of indifference and apathy.

She had a girlfriend from the army with whom she sometimes went out. They had gone together to a discotheque a few nights before, and she had danced for hours. She hardly knew how her lungs had held out. She told the therapist that it was stupid to dance like that. What for? The therapist told her that her dismissive gesture seemed much like a flag. Kate smiled, half agreeing.

She said that a psychologist would surely think that her problems came from her family, especially from her mad father (the therapist was acquainted with the family for she had treated Kate's mother). She thought this stupid, however and would hear nothing about her stupid family. At home she did what she wanted (meaning nothing), as she had done at school and in the army.

Kate's mother had come to therapy two years previously. She had been viciously beaten by Kate's father the night before and showed the therapist the ugly marks of his blows. With the therapist's encouragement, she had complained to the police for the first time after years of physical abuse. This proved enough to curb her husband's physical violence. Kate's mother later cancelled the complaint and though he still raved and cursed, he never hit her again.

The father was a tyrant. Kate's mother did his typing for him and whenever he found something not to his liking (which was often) he would yell at her and call her names, driving himself into a paroxysm of fury that, in the past, had often ended in blows. There were three children (Kate was the youngest). The father had planned to have five or six, but since each child proved to be flawed (the eldest had a long nose, the middle one had crooked legs, and Kate had asthma), he had decided that nothing good could be expected from the mother's rotten genes.

The family was abused both mentally and physically. If, for instance, someone sneezed or coughed in the father's presence, he would start yelling that they were doing it on purpose; if someone said a word about "grandmother" (who had been been confined to a mental hospital when Kate was 10 and was never visited or mentioned ever since), the father would punish the culprit most harshly. There were stranger things. The whole family had to visit the toilet one after the other in the morning. To save water, the toilet would be flushed once after everyone had finished. If someone felt the need to go to the toilet during the day, she had to warn the other family members, so that they might go as well.

Kate was the only one who dared to attend to her physical needs unannounced.

The therapist brought Kate's case to a consultation with one of the authors after two treatment sessions. She found Kate's condition alarming and felt paralyzed by her cynicism. It seemed impossible even to mention a positive goal: Kate would pour scorn on any offer of help or expression of sympathy. Cynics thus inure themselves against the very support they most need. Her cynicism would have to be addressed or no therapy could develop. However, neither a purely confrontative nor a purely supportive approach would do. Kate could be trusted to reject out of hand any demanding description and to ridicule any totally acceptant one. The following therapeutic split was thereupon framed:

"You have a strange kind of power: the power to paralyze. You have succeeded in paralyzing the workings of powerful institutions: the school, the army, and the dictatorship to which your family is subject. It took you only two sessions to paralyze me, too. How do you do it? You emit a constant noise that disqualifies, disables, and cripples any intention or initiative. You were right to think that I was going to connect this to your father. I was almost convinced by your noise machine not to do so. But it was precisely this noise machine that allowed you to keep your wits under your father's tyranny. How? Whenever you were faced with your father's crazy demands, you would make a lot of noise, endless noise, and end up not being crazy like him. You knew that listening to him and bending to his wishes would finish you. So you learned to emit this noise to keep him at bay. You are the only one at home who can lie in bed and go to the toilet at will. When he opens his mouth, your noise shuts him up. You have disqualified the disqualifier.

The noise, however, spills over and paralyzes you, too. It cancels your own wishes and plans. Even good feelings are dissolved. If you enjoyed dancing at night, the noise machine cancels the experience, retroactively. You are like Medusa who paralyzed by her look. When Perseus came, he kept looking backwards, while his polished shield reflected Medusa's staring into her own eyes. The paralyzer, like you, became paralyzed.

Your noise often takes the form of cynicism. Cynicism is an acid that eats up every living thing in your proximity. I told you that your cynical remarks looked like a flag to me. Actually they are more like an anti-flag, for whenever a flag is raised you will be sure to bend it.

We must recognize the value of your noise machine if we want to do anything about it. If we can see the positive side, we can also understand where it goes wrong. It has gone wrong in becoming so deeply ingrained, so much a part of your nature that your very face tends to contract in a dismissive spasm and become frozen in a disqualifying mask. Your hands, your eyes, your voice, everything gets caught in this stiff automatism. I want to work with you. I respect your power and your survivorship. I cannot, however, accept your veto over my activity. I cannot accept that there are areas where I am not supposed to touch. If I allow you to paralyze me like your father tried to paralyze you, the therapy will be worthless. For your sake, there can be no paralyzing in this room. Only then will we be able together to find your true rebel's face under your cynical mask."

Kate cried profusely and remained speechless for quite a while. She said it was all true. She wanted this kind of therapy. In a few weeks, however, nothing remained of this promising beginning. Kate had become even more inactive at home and more dismissive in the sessions. She disqualified the therapist as being unable to treat her (Perhaps only a genius could treat me and you are not one), and as not really devoted to her (If you really cared for me you would see me without pay and for many hours a day). She dismissed the therapy as a waste of money (How can we spend so much on talking, when children are dying of hunger in Africa?). She disparaged others, her friends especially, for being stupidly concerned with trivia. She soon stopped coming. The therapist tried to reach her by phone, but to no avail: she would not renew the therapy. Two months after this negative conclusion, the therapist asked us for a second consultation. She knew from the mother that Kate was spending more and more time in bed. Kate seemed to be in a profound clinical depression. Various group members raised the possibility that Kate might be helped by medication. The problem was how to present this option so that Kate might consider it. It was decided to raise the possibility of medication at the conclusion of a new therapeutic split to be sent to Kate as a letter:

"This letter is not an attempt on my part to renew the therapy. I respect your decision to end it. However, I have thought a lot about you and would like to share with you some of my ideas.

"I thought about the crucial role that your sense of specialness plays in your life: you feel and are special. You will not belong to any framework, you will not be chained, you will not be attached. You showed this at school, in the army, and of course, at home. Had you not felt this way, you would already have succumbed to your father, like others in your family. Today, also, your sense of specialness plays a role, offering, in the midst of despair, a partial consolation. In our sessions whenever we touched upon your specialness your face would beam and your voice would ring more sonorously. I believe that in those moments you felt most alive.

"Your specialness has another side, however; it is linked to your noise machine, for you feel special in proportion to your dismissal of others. This brings you under a new kind of tyranny, the tyranny of specialness, according to which whoever is not special has no right to exist: your family, your friends, myself, even you (when you stop feeling special) have no right to exist. Deeds, also, unless they are the works of a genius, have no right to exist. The tyranny of specialness thus voids the world and deprives you of the courage to be. Ironically, the very specialness that liberated you from the toilet-tyranny of your father has instituted another tyranny in its stead.

"I do not think, however, that this must be so. Your sense of specialness should be a source of vitality. I believe that it has turned sour because of a very stupid reason: you have become depressed. Your constant fatigue, your sleepiness, your lack of initiative, your inability to persevere, your crying, and your black view of things may well be the result of the physiological condition of depression. It would be an awful irony of fate if you were to waste your life sleeping and in misery, not because life is worthless, but because some preventable disregulation of your body makes it seem so. I want you to know that you can receive medication that will in all probability put an end to your depression. Your life-story would be the saddest story ever if all that is special within you should be buried, simply because you became physiologically depressed and were not physiologically treated.

"Again, this letter is not meant to renew the therapy. However, I will take the liberty of phoning you to see how you are doing. You should, of course, also feel free to call."

As a final twist to the story, the letter had not yet been mailed when the therapist received a call from Kate. She said once again that psychological treatment was an unaffordable luxury when children were dying of hunger, but might not perhaps some anti-depressant medication be of any help to her? The therapist replied that she had just finished writing her a letter, precisely on that issue. Thus did fate ratify with its ironical seal the therapist's attempt at participative persuasion.

2

CHARACTERS

In the past, a whole gallery of psychopathological types was available for the practitioner to draw from in depicting the client. Needless to say, such characterization usually fails to pass the test of narrative empathy. Clients can hardly recognize themselves in these types and even if they do it is usually to their detriment. Furthermore, psychopathological descriptions can no longer be justified as they had been by the assumption that they are objectively true. Many psychotherapists now tend to think differently: a psychopathological characterization is a construction as much as any other and far from helping the client, may actually become a crucial link in a pathologizing process.

Why then characterize at all? Would it not be better to keep an empty and open mind and to cultivate a therapeutic attitude of not-knowing (Goolishian and

Anderson 1987)? Does not the very attempt to characterize become a damaging and fixating endeavor? Our position in this and the following chapters follows from the assumption that we cannot help characterizing. We never meet a person without telling ourselves who she may be. Not to characterize would mean not to extrapolate from one act to the next and to be ready to have our clients, friends, relatives, and even ourselves, respond at any moment with any behavior whatsoever. We should then expect love, indifference, or murder from anyone, with base-rate probabilities.

Characterization is thus ubiquitous. The question is: What kind of characterization will it be?[1] It is our belief that we can oppose the client's negative self-descriptions or our own tendency to pathologize only by developing an alternative, fully humanizing, characterization: rather than finding fault with the client, we should celebrate her. It may be a new bias, but we would rather talk of *heroic* than of *neurotic* characters. The difficulty, however, is that our minds have been trained to perceive the latter, rather than the former. Anyone who has ever been exposed, for instance, to the types described in David Shapiro's *Neurotic Styles* (1965) cannot help seeing this person as hysteric, that one as obsessive, and that other one as paranoid.[2] Indeed, to

1. Therapists sometimes think they can use psychopathological concepts without causing damage if they keep such concepts to themselves. Psychopathological terms are thus a matter for supervision or case discussions, but not for the therapy. We think this position untenable: our views about the client transpire through our acts.

2. David Shapiro is the Charles Dickens of clinical characterization. He not only created an indelible gallery of types, but also

counter these prototypes we must develop a new gallery of psychotherapeutic heroes. In what follows, we shall try to make a modest contribution to this emerging typology by portraying three heroic styles: the romantic, the picaresque, and the epic. In fact, besides viewing these characters differently, we also find ourselves talking to them differently. Nothing would be more mistaken, however, than to think that first we identify the client's style and then decide how to talk to her. Rather, it is in conversing with the client that the characterization emerges. We might even say that as we learn to talk with the client, we begin to sketch out who she may be. In describing our three illustrative characters, therefore, we will also be describing the styles of conversation in which we find ourselves involved.

ROMANTIC STYLE

Intensity of feeling is the romantic's touchstone. Exaltation is the criterion of joy, rapture of love, and agony of pain. Life is worthwhile only if it is lived for the sake of absolute salvation and at the risk of absolute loss. Every moment is a potential crisis or epiphany, an intersection between time and eternity. No wonder that for the outsider the spectacle may seem overblown.

---

established a major criterion for character construction: the client's style should be so portrayed that any of his acts, no matter how bizarre, appears as the only plausible thing to do. In this respect he was a pioneer and a major forerunner of narrative empathy. In his emphasis on neurotic styles, however, he was true to his time.

What is felt as romantic excess often incites the desire to cure it so as to bring the affected individual back to the pale of reality. Common sense and moderation, however, are powerless with the possessed. Go convince a suicidal, love-spurned adolescent that the future holds adequate reparation for his ills, or a transported mystic to take care of her family, or a starry-eyed lover that his beloved has not the best credentials for a wife and a mother. We must give up our reasonable conceits if we want to reach the romantic. We must learn to follow the inner logic of the romantic, developing as we go an empathic narrative and characterization.

Abrams, the great literary historian and critic, coined the expression *natural supernaturalism* (1971) to designate the romantic's infusion of the natural world with the intensity of religious experience. This striving for fervor, Abrams argued, reflects a sense of lack and loss, which the romantic perceives with special acuteness, but to which we are all heirs. The romantic is highly sensitive to the trivialization of life that is the inevitable consequence of habit. Our mind is dulled and our vision dimmed with routine acts and sights. The romantic is the one who will not put up with this condition. For her, the coarseness of habit is a perpetual scandal. She protests, moreover, against our alienation from ourselves, others, and nature, a triple estrangement that is felt as a fall from an original unity. For her, there is hope in our very sense of loss, for it proves that our condition was not always so. Forgetting is the archbetrayal and nothing is more valuable than those intimations and recollections of our once undivided state, of the lost paradise of childhood, of our primordial sense of vital attachment, of what was once the splendor in the grass and the glory in the flower.

A similar positive yearning may be at work in those of our clients who seem perversely to cherish their suffering or embrace the guilt of past misdeeds. Such fixed ideas have illustrious antecedents: Augustine stole a pear and Wordsworth a rowboat and both suffered immensely for their crimes. For both, however, life gained meaning through their embracement of sorrow, for it guaranteed their continuing humanity. As long as they could feel the pain, not all was lost.

To do therapy with a romantic, we must learn to view their suffering with their eyes, as a necessary station in the life journey. It is not, however, the end station. As Abrams has argued, the spiritual autobiography of the romantic follows an almost fixed sequence through the stations of fall, exile, awakening, conflict, conversion, and salvation. The terms are similar to those by which the great religions depict the cosmic cycle from creation to millenium. Abrams argues that this is no mere coincidence: romanticism is actually a lay religiosity. Furthermore, just as in the religious cosmic cycle the end coincides with the beginning (the millenium is paradise regained), in the spiritual autobiography the final stage is a recovery of the lost origin. The pilgrimage is circular: Where are we going? asks Novalis, Always home (Abrams 1971, p. 390).

This yearning for origins has given occasion to descriptions of the romantic as sick and immature. Indeed, the romantic dreams of losing oneself in a supraindividual transport, to sink in an all-embracing reality, to fuse with the other, the all, or the void. Even death and suicide become ennobled as embodiments of this total wish. This morbidness, however, can be more than balanced by the romantic's affirmation of life. Take, for instance, Schiller's *Ode to Joy*, a celebration of the life power that binds us to each other and to nature, which brought from the deaf and ailing Beethoven an outburst of symphonic verve that has turned generations of placid concertgoers into raving dionysiacs.

Ruffle the feathers of a plaintive romantic nightingale and you are bound to find a lark. The same transformation occurs in the clinic. The bleakest ideation suddenly gives way to enthusiastic affirmation. The romantic is fervently alive even when he muses about dying. It helps the therapist to know this and it helps the client to have it pointed out. This brings us to another characteristic of the style—its dialectical polarity. Romantics delight in antithetical pairs: Paradise Lost/Paradise Regained, Hell/Heaven, Birth/Death, Lowly/Sublime. Oxymorons abound: the glory of the commonplace, the burning fountain, the supreme import of the trivial, and the heroic grandeur of the meek. A veritable gem in this line of thought is the esoteric name of one of Carlyle's heroes: *Diogenes Teufels Droeckh* (God-Engendered Devil-Shit). The romantic's life odyssey is, similarly, a rollercoaster of blessings and cataclysms. No repose is final: even redemption teeters continuously on the edge of a new turn of the spiral.

Of course, no discussion of the romantic can omit love. The romantic's love (which is quite different from what we mean colloquially by romantic love) can be viewed from an individual or from a cosmic perspective. Individually, love is the yearning for the object of the quest, variously symbolized as erotic attachment, maternal embrace, home, or the grail. In the great creations of the romantic mind, the symbols are fused together. Tristan's love in Wagner's opera, for instance, is simultaneously a longing for Isolde, for his dead mother, for his homeland, for an aboriginal realm of darkness, and for the abrogation of convention. The attachment to the beloved thus becomes so charged with multiple meanings that giving it up is tantamount to an absolute grounding of existence.

The second romantic perspective on love is as a cosmic force, the cohesive bond that keeps humanity and the world from fragmenting. This idea, everpresent in western thinking from the time of the pre-Socratic philosophers, reached what is perhaps its fullest expression with Plotinus and the neo-Platonists. Cosmic history, in this view, begins with an overflow of divine love that gives rise to the created world and proceeds through the yearning of all creation to return to the source. Human love is a particle of this cosmic longing. The love between human beings, the love of beauty, the love of truth, and the love of goodness are, as immortalized in Socrates' speech in the "Symposium," a series of rungs in the ladder that lead back to the origins. The romantic experience is an attempt to join this universal dance. When the romantic loves, the stars move in their orbits, because through love the individual enters the cosmic procession. Freud was thus not alone in viewing Eros as the principle that moves and unifies the world. Indeed, there are few who can withstand the lure of these eternal ideas.

The Mind of a Totalist

Ron came to me for help after a trip to India. The peak events of his trip were his encounters with eastern spirituality and with Indian families. Ron had worked as a volunteer in kindergartens and taught arithmetic to Tibetan children. He also became a brotherly mentor to an Indian child, returning again and again to visit her, teaching her, buying her clothes, and bringing her toys. Through Buddhist teaching he discovered compassion. He returned to Israel imbued with a sense of meaning and purpose. To his consternation this feeling gradually waned. Once again he was plagued by indecision. He tried to study psychology and anthropology but both were a far cry from the living reality he had just experienced. He came to me because I had been to India many times and had lectured on Tibetan Buddhism.

He told me of his previous therapy occasioned by his disappointment with himself in his first love. His girlfriend, perfection incarnate in his eyes, had grown so dependent on him that she would not let a day go by without endless phone calls and extraordinary meetings. He could not study or meet with other friends. He had to devote himself absolutely to her. Finally, he broke with her but soon became depressed because he had betrayed love. He had been guilty of a double crime: he had hurt another human being and had put his own advantage before love. He suffered terribly, considered suicide, and spent hours atop a cliff, waiting for the courage to take the plunge. He spent days alone in the desert alternating between misery and ecstasy. He would return with his backpack filled with colored sand from which he created compositions that embodied for him the marriage of the soul and the desert.

His first therapist helped him by refusing to offer

cheap consolation: he never tried to convince him as did others that he had done the only reasonable thing in parting from a girl whom they saw as sick; neither did he tell him that it was high time to stop grieving and start living. He respected Ron's pain, viewing it as an aspect of his personal integrity.

A few years before these events, Ron had experienced another crisis. Bad fighting had erupted between his parents, shattering their harmonious family. Ron's memories of the times when his immediate family would go together to his grandparents' on special occasions embodied for him all the good in the world. When the parents divorced and the holidays with the grandparents stopped, Ron felt exiled from paradise.

One more rift was added to these on his return from India. Buddhism and Judaism seemed to be radically opposed. This conflict symbolized for Ron all other incompatibilities. For him, union and disunion were all-embracing. Philosophical and personal discord were equally dismaying. He thought that if he could only bridge the gap between Jewish and Buddhist values, his life energies would resume their flow.

Talking to Ron, I soon found out that I would lose him if I were to concentrate on psychological issues to the detriment of moral and spiritual ones. Ron would become engaged in therapy only if he could respect me as a spiritual mentor. The romantic and religious language of the soul's pilgrimage served us well. In this language personal problems are described as stages in the journey, interpretations are dressed in parables, and therapeutic ideas are backed by examples from the lives of seekers and saints. I told him:

"You have been wounded in the past in the two areas that were most important for you: love and family. The wounds have slowly turned to scars, but not all is back to normal. Whenever strong emotions affect you, the scars bleed again.

"Some time ago, I talked to a friend who owns a factory. I complained to him that in Israel there are no mastercraftsmen with a tradition behind them as existed in countries with a more continuous history. He disagreed and told me a true story. Years before, he had imported a number of weaving machines from Germany. One of them broke down; the engine block was cracked. He took the engine to different places to have it fixed, but all said that the block could not be soldered. Time was crucial for his business was just getting started. He then heard of a man in Jerusalem whose technical genius had saved his life in a Nazi concentration camp and who was believed able to fix anything. My friend went to Jerusalem, found the man working in a garage, and brought him over to have a look at the engine. He looked very small beside the big machine. He examined it with care, ran his fingers gently over the crack, clicked his tongue, as if in pity, and mumbled, "Maybe mnmnmnmnmn . . . sew?" My friend asked what he was saying and he answered that he was just thinking aloud. He called my friend two days later and told him that the block could not be soldered but perhaps could be sewn. He proposed to drill small holes on each side of the crack, insert steel wires through the holes and tighten all up with a special machine he knew where to get. He hoped the repair would hold until a new machine arrived from Germany.

"The solution sounded crazy but since the man asked for very little money, my friend agreed. For a week the craftsman came to the factory every evening, all the way from Jerusalem, and spent long hours drilling and threading with infinite patience. When he was through he asked my friend to start the machine. The engine coughed and the machine began to work. The repair held for twelve years, longer than all the other machines in the batch. The *meister* sometimes came in to see how his baby was doing. He would have coffee with my friend and tell stories about great machines and strange repairs he had known. This, Ron, is what we have to do together; we have to sew your engine so that it may hold under pressure."

My diagnosis was warmly accepted, not in the least because of its very improbability. Thereupon, we agreed on some preparatory work consisting of physical exercise and meditation. Soon, we came to the areas where Ron felt his scars were most susceptible to strain: sex and anger. He felt that these areas were his greatest obstacles to spiritual advance. Overcoming these perceived obstacles was particularly important for Ron, because Judaism and Buddhism agreed for once in viewing sex and anger as dangerous. He was extremely annoyed with himself for failing to suppress them completely. I said:

"Though I am not an authority in spiritual matters, I think that you are making a mistake. You believe that Buddhism requires you to be free from anger and sexual desire. This is a distortion of the Buddhist position. True, this is the final goal, but it took the Buddha himself 20,000 life cycles to achieve what you are trying to do in three months! Perhaps you are afflicted with pride, even more than with sex and anger! You are wrong in yet another way because it is impossible to get rid of anger by getting angry that you are angry. The same is true for sexuality. Let me tell you the story of Milarepa.

"Milarepa was the devoted pupil of Marpa. After twelve years of strenuous spiritual training, Marpa sent Milarepa away to continue on his own. Milarepa went to live in a cave and one cold winter night three horrible demons invaded his cave. They shrieked, made faces, talked lewdly, tore his pictures, burned his books, spat on the mandala. Milarepa cast spells, called holy names, asked for his master's help, but all in vain. Heartbroken, he went out into the snow. He felt the demons were about to drag him to hell. Slowly, he started to think: This is the moment I've been waiting for. I've always wanted to rid myself of attachment. If those demons make me fear for myself then all my work has been in vain. A great calm fell upon him. He went back to the cave and saluted the demons, 'Honorable demons! Welcome to my humble abode. I know it is your appointed task to destroy me and drag me to hell. I don't want to prevent you from trying to fulfill it. As for me, my task is to strive for enlightenment. Let each of us try to perform his task to the best of his ability. Let us sit and talk about wisdom, you with your black dharma and I with my white dharma. But first, have tea with me.' The demons shrieked, bared their fangs, and lashed their tails. Milarepa repeated his invitation. Gradually, they shrank until they disappeared altogether.

"What you are doing, Ron, is trying to get rid of your demons by spells and imprecations. That will not work. Speak to your anger and sexuality like Milarepa: Welcome, honorable demons! Otherwise they will not leave you. The first stage is to accept the presence of your urges so that you may come to know them. You will find that some of them are more reasonable, others less. Only after inviting them for tea will you be able to let them go."

Ron took it upon himself to become acquainted with both his anger and his sexuality. He gradually grew more specific and told me of past actions that filled him with shame. The most painful, by far, was the memory dating from his early teens of having tortured a cat to death and tempting a younger boy to join him. He felt that he had displayed unspeakable cruelty and corrupted another child as well.

I told Ron that according to the values we both subscribed to, he *had* commited a great sin and that minimizing it would only add to the iniquity. (Later on Ron told me that he had feared I would try to get him off cheaply.) I told him of the Buddhist distinction between guilt and repentance. Guilt fixes the sinner in the past but the past can never be altered. Guilt does play a role, however, in purifying the sinner and paving the way for repentance, which is the sinner's forward-looking attempt to make reparation for the evil he committed. I told Ron he had been suffering from guilt and that our goal was to build upon his guilt so as to transform it into repentance. As Yom Kippur, the Jewish Day of Atonement, was approaching, I made use of the occasion to send him a letter with an implied therapeutic split:

"Yom Kippur is the time for moral reckoning and you have a serious sin to reckon with. However immoral may have been the *act* that you've committed, your *attitude* towards it is moral. I believe you have reached the right attitude by means of your guilt and your attempts at purification. You have purified yourself by suffering and by the help you gave to children. Maybe your whole year in India was one great unconscious attempt at purification. As the Jewish saying goes:

'Those who have never sinned cannot aspire to sit with the penitent.'

"I believe the time is ripe for your guilt to be finally transformed into repentance. This change is closely linked to your attempt to discover your practical and spiritual vocation. I think you are searching for a vocation that will allow you to spread good and reduce evil. Maybe your sin was part of a general plan for your life. Maybe you had to go through inner hell so as to know how much you desire the good. However, I don't think your offense can be obliterated. A stain will remain but, hopefully, pale and circumscribed. The good that stems from awareness of the stain, however, may spread on and on."

Ron attributed significance only to peak (or bottom) experiences. He became perplexed whenever he found himself emptied of exaltation. Prosaic states of mind were, for him, proofs of spiritual failure. For instance, he had never had a sexual relationship and he viewed sex as acceptable only if it were combined with perfect love in a completely sublime experience. Not a very helpful expectation for a young man. I tried to find a place for the commonplace in his worldview:

"The gray is part of life and not only a necessary evil. You can only enjoy walking if you give full attention to flatlands, valleys, and hillocks. Pinnacles do not stand alone. It would be a boring world if they did. I think that you lack courage for the worldly and the mundane. Without these, the holy and the spiritual have no connection to life. You expect, for instance, to experience love only as a total experience. Overweening pride, once again! I would wish you, on the contrary, to approach love and intimacy from the flawed, the human, perhaps the all-too-human, side."

Therapy became a battle for the matter-of-fact and the run-of-the-mill. I invoked all the saints and gurus in praise of human imperfection. The final story in this batch was that of the two lamas who had founded the Buddhist monastery where I had studied. Lama Zoppa stood for relentless self-demands and frightened his pupils with dire images of damnation. Salvation could only be attained through endless, unflagging self-exertion. Lama Ieshi would come in after Lama Zoppa's lectures and smile as he described the pleasures of meditation and the freshness of a beginner's fumbling attempts. There was always occasion to make things right by a good action. When Lama Ieshi died, the pupils could no longer study with Lama Zoppa. They missed Lama Ieshi's salt of fallibility that alone had made Lama Zoppa's teachings palatable. Things were redressed, however, when Lama Zoppa slowly integrated into his way some of the mildness of Lama Ieshi.

Ron was moved. He said with a wry smile: I am the offspring of the school of Shammai[3] with Lama Zoppa. This first glimmer of self-irony was a great therapeutic gain. Ron had not only poked fun at himself; he had done so by joining together the Jewish and the Buddhist traditions.

(Abrams' characterization of the romantic's natural-supernaturalism matches the tone and style of this therapeutic dialogue. The therapist felt from the beginning that Ron would not respond to a rationalist stance. He chose, therefore, to speak in parables sprinkled with quaintness and paradox. The initial story in which the cracked engine is sewn embodies this penchant towards

---

3. There were two great schools in the development of Jewish law: the school of Shammai, strict and austere, and the school of Hillel, soft and forgiving.

the absurd. The constant use of dual concepts and therapeutic splitting, for instance: immoral acts/moral attitude; guilt/repentance; Lama Ieshi/Lama Zoppa resonated well with Ron's romantic polarity. Additionally, the therapist's acceptance of the implied role of a spiritual mentor who did not flinch from a measure of tutorial harshness, for instance, in chastising Ron's inordinate pride—fits well with the romantic's concept of a spiritual pilgrimage with its incumbent load of sin and suffering.)[4]

PICARESQUE STYLE

The *pícaro* (meaning *rogue* in Spanish) is a tragicomic figure who, obliged to fend for himself in a hostile world and endowed with wits and a strong will to live, develops the essential virtues of the survivor: cunning and duplicity. The pícaro is no mere survivor, however. The society that educates him is characterized by a double standard of morality. Honesty, generosity, and honor are extolled, but the prize goes to those who only make a show of these qualities. The pícaro must, therefore, learn how to wear the right mask at the right time. The show of nobility and goodness is more important than the substance. Society's professed values slip in, however, and whenever he encounters living

4. Some of the cases in this book are interspersed with comments in italics. These comments are different from those that appear in regular type as part of the case: the italics reflect our post-hoc perpective as authors of *Constructing Therapeutic Narratives*; the comments in regular type reflect the perspective of the therapist or consultant in charge of the case.

examples of positive humanity, the pícaro enters on a course of inner vacillation. He may then not only show generosity, but feel it, and care not only for the mask of honor, but for its heart. These positive human impulses, however, are in constant battle with the deceitfulness inculcated by his education. Thus torn by conflict, the pícaro develops a gnawing need to justify himself, both in his own eyes and before others (Bjornson 1977).

The pícaro emerged from folklore into literature in the sixteenth century with an anonymous work that became one of the earliest bestsellers: the fictional confessions of *Lazarillo of Tormes*. Lazarillo was sent by his mother into the world, armed with one short piece of advice: *Vale-te por ti*, an injunction meaning both "Watch out for yourself and be worth your mettle." He showed his will to live when he first met with a funeral procession. He ran like mad to the home of the blind beggar whom he served, bolted the door, and pressed his body against it, so that death might not enter.

Lazarillo was soon to find out that he really had to watch out for himself. The blind beggar asked him to look closely at a bull-shaped stone and as Lazarillo approached it the beggar knocked his head against it, to teach him he had to prove sharper than the devil. This initiation was the prelude to a series of battles of wit between Lazarillo and his master. Lazarillo began stealing wine from the beggar's bottle. The beggar countered by keeping the bottle in his hands. Lazarillo inserted a straw and sipped the wine from a distance. The beggar corked the bottle with his thumb. Lazarillo drilled a hole in the bottle and crawled underneath, letting the wine trickle into his mouth. The beggar waited for Lazarillo to lie snugly under the bottle and then smashed it on his face.

His next master, a priest, gave Lazarillo valuable lessons in hypocrisy. In the presence of others, he would make a show of generosity by giving Lazarillo the key to the larder. In reality, however, Lazarillo was allowed no more than one onion every three days. After the priest, Lazarillo served a squire who was also a past master at impression management. From him, however, Lazarillo learned a deeper lesson. Once when they got hold of a gold coin, the squire did not keep it to himself, but sent Lazarillo to buy food so that the two might eat like counts. This was Lazarillo's first experience of companionship (*com* = *with, pane* = *bread*, in Latin).

Lazarillo's "education" proved successful. He grew into a proficient mask wearer. He finally reached a modicum of security by marrying a bishop's mistress, thus providing the illicit affair with a cover. In this role of paid cuckold, however, Lazarillo felt ill at ease. To justify himself he wrote a long letter to a high church dignitary (the book that we have been reading) telling his bitter life story. Or, should we view this confession only as another mask, by which Lazarillo tries to look better in his own and the world's eyes? This ambiguity is inherent to the pícaro's existence. Self-justification is always a burning issue for him and the question always remains whether the face that is revealed in the apology is not just another mask.[5] Indeed, truth and falsehood,

5. Picaresque heroes from Lazarillo through Defoe's Moll Flanders, Grimmelhausen's Simplicius, Le Sage's Gil Blas, Mann's

self-revelation and impression-management can hardly be separated in the life of the pícaro.

We often recognize the pícaro in the clinic through his lies or his inflated attempts at impression-management. The self-image that the pícaro attempts to sell, however, is one with which he would fain identify and to which he feels he will soon be entitled. So much so that to his mind he may not be strictly lying, but merely taking an advance on future dues. The therapist often reacts either by confronting him or by inquiring into his need to impress. In both cases, the therapist takes a stand on the side of what she views as reality. There, however, is precisely where she may go wrong. The pícaro has had enough of reality. He became what he is precisely because his whole life has been an endless clash with reality. When we confront the pícaro with reality, we are having recourse to an external rather than an empathic narrative, pointing out to him the absurdity of his behavior, feeling sure, all the time, that in his place we would have behaved quite differently. Little wonder that he finds himself even more estranged. Consider the following example.

Too Much Reality

> A young man came to one of the authors years ago, in an attempt to save his marriage. His wife and his parents-in-law had lost all trust in him. He had lied profusely, not for concrete advantages but more to gain

---

Felix Krull, Le Carre's Pym, Bellow's Augie March, to a host of other less-known figures, always present themselves to us through an apologetic confession.

their respect. For instance, in order to seem a successful real estate dealer he would often tell them that a deal was closed before it was. He invariably exuded charm from every pore, confident that success was just around the corner. His gifts were invariably stunning—the most beautiful of flower bouquets or exquisite delicatessen. He dressed his son like a prince. He was a born aristocrat if ever there was one. Fate might delay but not deny him recognition.

His existence was a series of falls and near escapes, threats and dodges, plights and stratagems, and always the miracle of staying afloat (or almost so) against all odds. The pretense of nobility reflected the desperation of his predicament. His life story was that of a typical pícaro. Rejected by his own family he had left home and country to try his luck in a distant land. He dreamt of acceptance, favor, and success. When he finally found himself warmly accepted by his fiancée's family, he just had to show that he was the noble scion they so richly deserved. How could time be such a laggard!

I tried to help him control his lying. I encouraged him to confess to his wife rather than take recourse in soothing subterfuges. We role-played his confessions to her and imagined the ensuing recriminations in detail. Alas, I was trying to dose him with reality. He was soon convincing *me* that he had a deal in his hands that would definitely make him. He knew I did not believe him, but I would soon find out he was as good as his word. We found ourselves enacting the same interactions he had with his parents-in-law. I pointed out the parallel, but he thought it obvious: of course my response was similar to theirs! He was sure, however, that truth would vindicate him. I tried to evade questions of truth and talked instead about his inner reality. He was impervious. Predictably, the famous deal failed to materialize. The sequel was very quick. In a matter of weeks he had left for still another country. I realized only much later that Don Quixote had been sitting in my office. Had I but recognized him!

But would it have made a difference? It might. Don Quixote is a character whose very excesses make us vibrate in sympathy. There is logic and nobility in his madness. He became immortal precisely for trying to bridge the gap between the ideal and reality with the bounty of his imagination. He was like my client harshly confronted by the followers of reality, and nowhere did he show more heroic stature than in withstanding the incredulity of the world while keeping his own faith intact. Perceiving the similarities between my ill-starred client and Don Quixote might have helped me construe an empathic narrative. The pain he was enduring and causing to his loved ones might have been embodied in a therapeutic split. The whole ensuing dialogue might then have been different.

Don Quixote, like our young man, often caused more ill than good to those he tried to help. One of those he saved pleaded, "If you meet me again, don't help me or assist me even though you see them cutting me to pieces, but leave me to my misfortune; it can't be worse than what will come from your worship's help" (*Don Quixote*, I, 31). Don Quixote would also, like my client, find lies to flesh out reality, when the power of delusion failed him. Thus, on his return from the Cave of Montesinos, Don Quixote told of meeting with the dead and of the marvels of the underworld (II, 23). Later on, when Sancho expatiated on his own sights from the flying horse, Clavileño, Don Quixote whispered in his ear, "Sancho, since you want me to believe what you have seen in the sky, I want you to believe what I saw in the Cave of Montesinos. I say nothing more" (II, 41). This confession did not diminish Don Quixote's stature in any wise (Torrance 1978).

Cervantes' *Don Quixote* was actually a variant of the picaresque novel. Indeed, the quixotic way offers a possibility of redemption for the pícaro, allowing him to dignify his shabby and downtrodden existence. By honoring my client's quixotic bent in all its redeeming absurdity, I might have changed a failing dialogue about reality and self-control into one about the larger meaning of his misadventures. I might have become his chronicler and, thus, a partner in his transmutation of a life of drabness into one of chivalry. We might both then have been surprised by his reserves of real nobility (see Omer 1994, pp. 57–60, for another quixotic hero).

To help the pícaro, we must find cause for celebration beyond the dreariness. Don Quixote, however, is surely not the only possible model; many clients would rather remain Lazarillos! Fortunately, other comic figures from folklore and literature are available to help us develop empathic characterizations for our pícaros. But one may rightly ask, should we help our clients mirror themselves in risible characters? Some exaltation! Indeed, the comic character was long considered to be of baser metal than the tragic or the epic one. Comedy, it was held since Aristotle, depicts humans as worse than they are and as immersed in the trivial. A comic *hero* would then be a contradiction in terms. This view was accepted by most philosophers and literati. From earliest times, however, a different perspective about the virtues of the comic flourished, far from the limelight of learning and respectability. The comic character was seen in this unofficial system as the embodiment of biological drive, fantastic freedom, dogged humanity, and belligerent selfhood virtues that brought him into inevitable clash with respectable society (Bakhtin 1984, Torrance 1978). He was the torchbearer of full-blooded vitality against limiting convention. Viewed from this angle, the comic character was truly a hero.

Along these lines, the therapist might perhaps develop an empathic narrative about the pícaro as a character teeming with outrageous exuberance. Outrage as a liberating gesture has a long and respectable lineage, such as the carnival king who turns society on its head, the courtly fool who is licensed to bite, legendary heroes such as Till Eulenspiegel and Robin Hood, and such inimitables as Falstaff and the good soldier Schweik. All of these are redeemed pícaros. Their capacity to inspire can be gauged by the whiff of freedom we experience when we are confronted with their age-old deeds. We believe that many a lowly pícaro who sat with us in the clinic, sulking over the dying embers of his small rebellion, could have been found worthy of a place, however modest, in this comic pantheon. He might feel justified if, ridding our eyes of professional sanctimoniousness, we recognized him for what he was: a day toiler in the order of Saint Falstaff and Saint Schweik.

With other pícaros, however, still another way must be found. Neither the flight of imagination nor the outrageous carnival will do for them. Their life becomes worthy, as Lazarillo's once did, in its priceless moments of companionship. This interplay of essential loneliness and miraculous togetherness has been immortalized by Chaplin's tramp. Indeed, the audience never believes that the tramp will live happily ever after with the adopted kid, the once-blind florist, or the wild girl of the streets. We all know, when we meet him again in the next film, that it is the same tramp we are viewing, alone again. We do not even ask what happened to his previous companions. Life, however, would be senseless without such encounters. It may well be one of the nobler tasks of a therapist to help her clients sanctify these meetings where they have been found worthy of giving and receiving real human warmth.[6]

Middle-Age Crisis

> Muli felt trapped in a net of relationships that allowed him no breathing space. He wanted to run away, emigrate, hide in the wilderness. He felt enormously tired. He had four sons by his wife, Orit, and two daughters by his mistress, Lee. He had kept this arrangement going only by dint of endless promises, lies, and pretense, telling the mistress to wait a little longer and the wife that all would be well in the end. In the last few months, Muli had also become entangled with a third woman and a fourth was waiting in the wings. There were further complications: Muli had gone through two bankruptcies and a series of false starts in the course of a few years. Presently, he was trying to develop a career as an insurance agent. During

6. One literary scholar claims that the peculiar hero of our age is precisely *the picaresque saint*, who transcends his meaningless wanderings by his moments of warm companionship (Lewis 1959).

his breaks from work, wife, lover, and kids, he would have a tryst with number three. No wonder he was tired!

He was a pícaro of long standing. Unable to raise him alone, his widowed mother had sent him to a kibbutz when he was 5. After his first shocking year alone, he gradually made a social niche for himself by assuming the role of funny fellow. He could always find the biting word or the droll tale to fit any occasion. His facetiousness earned him facile friendships but also got him in trouble. He was once dropped from a diplomatic course because of his irreverence. Later on he added a gallant's charm to his social assets. Even during his first interview, he displayed this special talent by flirting with the attractive interviewer. The staff decided to assign him a male therapist.

Muli's efforts as a wit and a Don Juan exemplified his usual dealings with the world. He would always try for the speedy conquest or the stunning gimmick, a style which in business at least proved disastrous: Muli repeatedly became involved in the most fantastic financial schemes, sometimes destroying at one stroke the fruit of years of labor.

In his unstable life, his relationship to his double family stood out in conspicuous contrast. He bustled, lied, and made business like a pícaro, but loved and cared like a father. He arranged birthday parties, kept in touch with teachers, put the young ones to bed and helped the older ones with their homework. Among the siblings from both mothers a warm relationship had developed. The in-laws from both sides cared for the children and Muli cared for them in turn.

With the therapist's help, Muli succeeded in a couple of months in putting an end to his third romantic entanglement. He also became more careful in business and signed an agreement with the therapist, committing himself not to engage in any financial venture without discussing it with him beforehand. This paved the way for the longest stretch of occupational and financial stability in Muli's career. The therapist, however, became concerned; he felt that Muli was losing his zest. Muli complained of the grayness and drabness of life. His future seemed to hang on an impossible choice between dull stability and picaresque anarchy. To make matters worse, both women had lately started to press for a decision or, at least, for a change in the status quo. Muli felt drawn once again to a course of false promises. The therapist consulted with us and the following message was delivered to Muli in the next therapy session:

"You view yourself as a bungling failure. It seems that you don't understand the uniqueness of your creation. According to all professional books, a double family like yours is a sheer impossibility. Your lifework proves them wrong: you have created the weirdest family garden I've ever seen. You invest body and soul in this garden, in your women, and in your children. The two pests that could destroy your lifework, other women and business gambles, you are now keeping at bay.There are other dangers, of course: Lee's and Orit's demands are far from harmless. However, your promises to them are no solution. They may postpone the crisis, but it will be worse when it comes. I think you should tell them of your love, but you should also tell them that you cannot give up any part of the family. I am willing to help you do this in a way they may accept."

Muli and the therapist developed the following message to be delivered to both women:

"You, our children, my other children, your parents, this whole family, are all my family—my precious family. It is a strange family, but if there are failings they are not in the areas of love and care. [To Lee:] You are my lover but Orit is the wife of my youth. I cannot turn my back on either of you. [To Orit:] I may have sown my wild oats, but I cannot turn my back on those for whom I am responsible. It would be inhuman to do so. [To both:] You are exceptionally dear to me. My love goes not only to you and the children but also to your parents. I love them as if they were my own. If, some day, you decide that you cannot go on with this, my world will be destroyed. I pray to God that you will not take this awful step. My loyalty is proved every day and every hour. I help and participate in everything, in keeping house, in raising the children, in caring for the larger family. My love and involvement do not vanish when I am with my other children and their mother. This is my destiny. This is the strange family that I have built but that I love with body and soul."

Both messages were treasured by Muli. They justified him as a person and honored him as a highly original creator. They helped him replace his evasive style by one of proud self-affirmation. He felt that he now had a better way to talk to Orit and Lee. The message to the two women also made a powerful impact; the urgency of their pressure diminished. Therapy gradually veered away from the need to protect him. Various sessions were spent depicting his unconventional achievements, and he stopped complaining about the drabness of existence. His financial stability allowed him for the first time to take all six children (without the mothers) together for a trip abroad. He dreamt of a huge Passover feast for the whole family.

EPIC STYLE

In his classic essay, "Odysseus' scar," Auerbach (1953) portrays the Homeric epic as a style of representation in which reality is fully externalized and illuminated;

nothing remains in the shade, no feelings are left unexpressed, and there are no inklings of unplummeted depths. Auerbach illustrates this description with the episode of Odysseus' scar: Odysseus returns home after an absence of twenty years disguised as a beggar. Penelope sends the housekeeper, Euryclea, to wash the stranger's feet. The old woman fetches the basin and the water, mixes hot and cold and reminisces about her absent master. Odysseus, meanwhile, remembering the scar on his thigh, moves back out of the light to avoid recognition. Euryclea, however, touches the scar and, startled, drops Odysseus' foot in the basin. Penelope, whose attention has been diverted by Athena, perceives nothing. At this point, the narrator inserts a long parenthetical remark, to tell us about the hunting incident in which Odysseus had sustained his wound. Still a youngster, Odysseus had gone for a visit to his grandfather Autolycus. The latter's domain and character, the exchange of greetings, the banquet before the hunt, the gathering of the hunters, the encounter between Odysseus and the boar, and the return to Ithaca, are leisurely described. The narrator then brings us back to Penelope's chamber, where the foot finishes falling and the water splashing. Every detail is depicted with the same careful attention. The same light illumines everything, fully and equally.

This universal luminosity is evident also in Homer's atmospheric settings. The simile that recurs most frequently in the *Odyssey* is that of dawn spreading its fingertips of rose. Light is ubiquitous. It brings the human closest to the divine:

> The sun rose on the flawless brimming sea
> into a sky all brazen all one brightening

for gods immortal and for mortal men
on plowlands kind with grain.
(*The Odyssey*, IV, 1–4)[7]

The heroes' minds, likewise, have no dark recesses. Their thoughts, wishes, and passions are open and direct. They behave decisively and without conflict. When one of the suitors begs for mercy, Odysseus swiftly cuts off his head. He glories in the immediacy of his acts.

Space, too, is ample and open. No epic is conceivable without a journey at its heart. Ithaca, Ilium, Hades, Scylla and Charybdis are a few of the famous stations in Odysseus' peregrinations. The breadth of the heroes' motions is a measure of the vastness of their souls. In this bright, wide world, the characters bustle about realizing to the full their grandeur and freedom. They are self-assured and at peace with themselves. Even their equipment is exalted, its quality and splendor an extension of their selves: their shields are their castles and their helmets shine like stars (Routh 1927). They ride magnificent horses, living symbols of beauty and mettle, who will not listen to any voice but that of their own charioteer. Xanthos and Balios, Achilles' famed steeds, weep copiously over the corpse of Patroclus.

But now, the reader might justly ask, what have these mighty beings in their divinely shared world to do with psychotherapy? When was Achilles last seen in the clinic? Indeed, clients do not come to us straight from

7. Robert Fitzgerald's translation, 1961, New York: Anchor Books.

the pages of the *Iliad*. However, the epic as an instrument of personal formation is highly relevant for psychotherapy. Let us explain.

The epics were not created for private reading but for singing and declamation (de Vries 1963). A courtly audience would listen to an epic singer at a banquet, or a gathering host before a battle. The recitation would awaken a spirit of emulation and instill bravery in the hearts of the knights. On rare occasions, someone might hear his own deeds celebrated in song. More usually, however, the listeners would find themselves drawn by the feats of others toward an ever receding horizon of grandeur. In the process some comfort would also accrue to their own sense of smallness and vulnerability. Nowhere is this more poignantly expressed than in the *Odyssey*. After being battered by the waves for days on end, the skin of his hands torn by pointed rocks, his body blown by winds and emaciated by hunger, cast out half-dead and naked on a distant strand, Odysseus is taken up unrecognized into a royal hall where a blind harpist sings of his feats at Troy. Odysseus covers himself with his mantle, vainly trying to hide his groans and tears from his host.

Like Odysseus, it is when we feel at our lowest that we are most in need of the epic. We then yearn for such a blind harpist. Epic poems are created for those who are challenged by superior odds: for the Frodos and the Telemachuses among us. The epic is thus an instrument of transformation. It strengthens and exalts us in the face of disaster, disease, cruelty, and bereavement. The same may be said of a psychotherapeutic conversation in epic style: it does not assume that we are inherently heroic. In our most fateful moments, however, it may help to bring out the heroic in us. It is the grandeur of the challenge and our acceptance of it that lends us an epic dimension. Indeed, the epic underscores our readiness to face up to fate, weak and vulnerable as we are. When Odysseus asks Kalypso to send him back home, the nymph asks him if his mortal wife can be more desirable or beautiful than she is. Odysseus replies:

> My lady goddess, here is no cause for anger.
> My quiet Penelope—how well I know—
> Would seem a shade before your majesty,
> death and old age being unknown to you,
> while she must die. Yet, it is true, each day
> I long for home, long for the sight of home.
> If any god has marked me out again
> for shipwreck, my tough heart can undergo it.
> What hardship have I not long since endured
> at sea, in battle! Let the trial come.
>
> (*Odyssey, V*).

Mortality is thus everpresent to the epic hero. It is not with a sense of invulnerability that Achilles sets forth on his final exploits, but in full consciousness that his end is near for he was doomed at birth to be cut off in the spring of life (*The Iliad*, XXIV). The epic hero thus embodies the paradox of vitality and acceptance in the shadow of death. The epic teaches us to live most fully, where we are most faced with our limits.

The epic hero is helped in this task by the community from which he partakes. *The Knights of the Round Table* and *The Fellowship of the Ring* are greater than the sum of their members and so are the family and the tribe. This is a different brotherhood from the companionship of underdogs who warmed the cockles of the pícaro's heart. Participation in the heroic family confers almost superhuman status. When Odysseus meets with the shade of Achilles sunk in the lethargy and despondency of death, he tells the dead man about the war feats performed by his son. Even in Hades, Achilles' spirit soars and his feet grow light:

> I said no more
> for he had gone off striding the field of asphodel
> the ghost of our great runner, Achilleus Aiakides
> glorying in what I told him of his son.
>
> (*Odyssey X*)

The very immensity of the forces poised against the heroes adds to their stature; they are uplifted by the majesty that defeats them. Thus, it is the rare hero who dies by mortal hands alone. Rather, it takes an offended deity to quench their flame. Nature also confronts them in its most daunting manifestations. The angry sea around their ships is like a cauldron seething over intense fire, heaving, rising, and shooting spume. The maelstrom that draws them makes the cliffs bellow all around and the dark sand rage in the deep (*Odyssey, XII*). Death and defeat, thus raised to cataclysmic proportions, redeem the falling from insignificance. No wonder the muses themselves sing at the hero's funeral.

This externalized discourse, however, seems rather foreign to psychotherapy. Most of us have been trained to favor internalized descriptions and explanations. We tend to view *in*trospection as a sign of maturity and *in*sight as a precondition of cure. This inner-oriented mode may turn even physical illness or natural disaster into the outward manifestations of psychological conflict. Internalization, however, does not preclude epic grandeur. In Jung's writings, for instance, life is depicted as a psychological odyssey in the course of which the individual grapples with the monsters and deities that have besieged humanity from time immemorial. Dreams, strivings, transitions, personal encounters are landmarks in this mythic journey. Thus, a client's whimsical trait may be translated in therapy into the sign of a calling. Suppression of the calling would turn the client's life, like that of the recalcitrant prophets of old, into a wasteland, a pile of dry stones, a morass of meaninglessness. The client/hero is helped to recognize the spiritual allies that may guide him towards the threshold that must be crossed. The crossing becomes a leap into darkness, symbolizing the client/hero's readiness to annihilate the old self (Campbell 1949).

Therapy thus comes to resemble the knightly hall in fostering a spirit of participation in the legendary. In Jungian therapy, however, the monsters and deities belong to the inner mind alone. They are the hidden corners of the soul. It was left to White and Epston (1990) to develop a style of therapeutic conversation, which instead of internalizing external events, *externalized* internal ones, thus bringing psychotherapy closest to Auerbach's (1952) major criterion of the epic.

White and Epston's externalization begins with the villain who is not a human but a personalized version of the client's problem. The naming of the problem is highly pertinent in this respect: Sneaky-Poo, The

Voices, The Monsters, Misery, and Dependence are some of the denizens in White and Epston's bestiary. There is no dragon, however, without a knight. Our narrative propinquities guarantee that, as the villain begins to fill the stage, the hero must be getting ready in the wings. The next therapeutic task is precisely to draw the picture of the client/hero. Such questions as: "How did you prepare yourself for this step?" "What did you do when younger that could provide some clue that this development was on the horizon of your life?" "How will this new picture of yourself change what you plan to do in the near future?" establish epic continuity. Hercules throttled snakes in his crib and young Arthur pulled swords from rocks. Clients and therapists grow in their conviction of the hero's destiny, as the tale is spun between past and future.

White and Epston also emphasize the public side of the client's narratives. They advise the client to tell others about her new life-decisions, award her titles for her exploits and ask her permission to inspire others with her tales. In a similar vein, the challenges and ordeals described in the following case became a source of inspiration to many a cancer patient, both during the heroine's life and after her death.

Let the Trial Come!

> Ofra[8] came forward when we asked for a volunteer in one of my courses to illustrate some hypnotic techniques for the treatment of anxiety. I interviewed her

8. All names and identifying details in this case are true. Ofra was glad to know, before her death, that we wanted to write up her case with full particulars.

before the class and she told us that she had had both her breasts removed because of cancer, in the course of the last three years. When the disease first appeared, she had decided she would never give up. She told everything to her adolescent children and showed them the scars of the first mastectomy. She told her therapy clients about her illness as well. Her style was to fight it out in the open; her combativeness, however, was tempered by a streak of lighthearted acceptance. For example, one of her typical gestures was a flick of the right hand upwards, which seemed to be saying: "So what?" or "So be it!" One month before her death she told me that everything was perfectly well. Then, she added, "Maybe I'll die . . ." and with a flick of her hand, "So what?" She liked to say that once in a while, God would tell his angels, "It's been quite a while since we last dealt with Ofra. High time to give her a knock on the head!" And she would smile and flick up her hand. She was ready to take on such an opponent.

In class Ofra asked for help in dealing with the surge of anxiety she always experienced before and during medical examinations, particularly the CT-scan, which had become in her eyes the harbinger of disastrous news. She had been hypnotized before and her visualizing ability was superb. In seconds she could bring herself to the top of a mountain, from where she surveyed the landscape. She seemed entranced by the beauty of the place. In the course of our later work, I came to understand that she always externalized inner events. Her imagery had a peculiarly spacious character. She derived strength from the ample vistas she invoked. In the session before the class, I made use of this ability to help her face the scan. I asked her to view herself flying above the examination room in which she was having the scan. I told her that from high up, she could *know* about the suffering in the room but *feel* the zest and the freedom of her flight. Little did I know that this duality between feeling and knowing, between coping and acceptance, would become the central theme of our therapy. She phoned me a few days later to tell me she had succeeded in distancing herself in flight during the scan. The results of the scan, however, were bad; part of her lung would have to be removed. She asked me to accept her as a client, to help her face the trial.

I often listen to music when I do hypnotic work. As I worked with Ofra preparing her for the approaching lung surgery, a Chopin nocturne was being played on the radio. Her face softened and she said, "Listen to the music. Nothing relaxes me more than piano music." I turned the radio louder. The music grew restless. Ofra began to cry, "I loved to play the piano as a child. One day, I came home from school and the piano wasn't there any more. My parents had sold it because it interfered with my studies. Fool that I was, I never went back to play. Now I know that I won't be able to play anymore." The music grew peaceful, again. I told her, "Listen, after the tempest and the pain there is a deep, positive calm. Who knows, maybe after the operation, you will find that the desire to play is coming back to you. Maybe your fight against the disease will teach you not to let others keep you from what you need. The better you fight, the more you'll want to play and the more you want to play, the better you'll fight." Music gave her a sense of touching base. I told her about Anthaeus, the giant, who drew strength from his mother, the earth, and was invincible as long as his feet were planted in it. I believe I wanted her to play, precisely because she thought it impossible (her mettle was proving contagious). And play she did. She played for most of the two years that were left to her, playing even when her fingers trembled with weakness.

Anthaeus' story was the first in a series I would tell while Ofra was in hypnosis. In particular, I used the stories to achieve a balance between hope and acceptance. Ofra knew the Simmontons' (1981) work on cancer and had decided that she would defeat the illness by the power of her mind. This inner resolution helped her through the initial stages of the malady. However, when she got worse she blamed herself for allowing the cancer to triumph.

Ofra's fighting spirit would have to be sustained *together* with her acceptance. So, I told her of the Roman generals, Fabius and Scipio, in their fight against Hannibal. Hannibal stood close to the gates of Rome. The republic, in all its might, was helpless against his advance. He had crossed the Pyrenees and spread his shadow over Italy. All the Roman generals, except old and wily Fabius, had been defeated. Knowing he could not vanquish Hannibal, Fabius avoided direct engagements, retreating slowly but keeping his army intact. This strategy earned him the scorn of the Romans. A Roman general who shuns battle? Roman pride could not abide this. He was not replaced, however, for no general could be found to take command. The only alternative was Scipio, who was young and inexperienced. Scipio declared that he would recruit and train a great army, but until it was ready, Fabius would have to stay on; it was impossible to build an army and fight at the same time. Under the cover of Fabius' retreat, Scipio built his force. When his time came, he was not only to expel Hannibal from Italy, but also to enter the very gates of invincible Carthage.

Ofra complained of the ravages of chemotherapy and, even more, of her weakness in facing its side-effects. At times, she would lose hope and think of giving up all medical treatment. She asked whether I could help her develop a hypnotic protective shield. I told her that not only I, but her the piano teacher, her husband, the children, the doctors, and the chemotherapy were her protective shield. As she entered hypnosis, I told her of a film I had seen: *Demolition Man* with Sylvester Stallone. Stallone is a cop who breaks all regulations in pursuit of an arch-criminal. As a result, he is sentenced to being frozen for many years as is the arch-criminal. Some fifty years later, the criminal is thawed by other criminals, whose chief he becomes. He wakes to a world devoid of violence; even dirty words are punished by a fine. The courteous police of this peaceful society are powerless against him. Somebody, however, remembers that there is a frozen cop who, in the past, knew how to deal with this arch-criminal. So, Stallone is also thawed. One of his first desires is to relieve himself. He asks where he can shit and is fined by the policemen. He asks what they are fining him for and they explain that he has uttered a dirty word. He says "Fuck!" five times and is given five fine slips, which he uses to wipe himself. People call him "The Cave Man." The expectable pursuit then begins, in the course of which Stallone destroys the city plumbing, blows up the museum, and accidentally causes the mayor's death (not much of a loss for he was a scoundrel). Still, he is the only one who can deal with the criminal and he finishes him in the end. Chemotherapy, I told Ofra, is your Demolition Man.

Ofra learned well how to get help from the Demolition Man. She would make use of the simile whenever she found herself trapped by her desire to overcome every obstacle by willpower alone. Calling the Demolition Man would then become emblematic of her acceptance of painful treatments. She wrote in her journal of this interplay between fighting and resignation. "At a given moment, instead of fighting on and on as a big hero, I became a tired woman, sick of battle. Paradoxically, this meeting with weakness liberated me. Something cleared up in my heart and the inner crying grew softer. While waiting for the results of the examinations, I no longer felt the need to work myself up. The anxiety simmered on, but bearably and quietly."

Ofra recovered and felt well for months. She became very active in helping other cancer patients. Her story became a powerful therapy for others. The act of telling it was a therapy for herself. She was liked and respected by the patients and the staff of various oncological and rehabilitation wards. Her case was described, in her presence, at two professional conferences. She pursued this activity for as long as she could stand on her legs.

Her behavior in hypnosis underwent a singular change. Previously, when dealing with pain, she would have me describe her as flying in an open landscape, looking down on the bustle or on her body far down, a bundle of pain, known but unfelt. Now, she no longer wanted to watch the people moving below. She preferred to remain in her detachment. I believe she was preparing for death. But still she fought on. Her physical condition worsened and she became bedridden. I searched for new images that could do justice to her sense of fate while still leaving room for hope. Hope and resignation, however, follow different time schedules; hope needs a longer time perspective, while resignation is an acceptance of the brevity of time. The combination of the two required a paradoxical time metaphor.

I told her of General Raful's battle in the Yom Kippur War. He had been in command of the northern division when the Syrians attacked massively. Time was crucial for the mobilization of Israel's reserve forces. His voice was heard again and again on the radio, calling to the fighters, "Hold on for five minutes!" This same message was repeated for hours. Soldiers told later on that they had been sure Raful knew that reinforcements were about to arrive (there weren't any for a long time). Slowly, the Syrian onslaught was contained. I later heard Raful telling what had been in his mind. In the War of Liberation, twenty-five years before, he had been in command of a small force in Jerusalem, surrounded by a vastly superior army. Half of his soldiers were wounded. He kept yelling, "Hold on for five minutes!" He knew, however, that the end was near. "Hold on for five minutes!" After four hours, the enemy retreated. They believed that such spirit could only be evinced by a force very sure of its fighting power. It seemed as if the five minutes of the War of Liberation had been endlessly lengthened, merging with the five minutes of the Yom Kippur War.

In her final weeks, Ofra was blind and could hardly move. I asked her what she now used to visualize on her own. She told me that she would view herself as victorious over the disease, a crown of laurels on her brow like the woman warrior on the statue "Citadel," she had seen in Budapest. I told her that she had already earned the crown and that, in my eyes, she would always remain the very image of the unconquerable citadel. On her last day, she could communicate only by finger movements. I asked her whether she wanted help with the anxiety or the pain. She smiled and found the strength to flick up her hand.

(Ofra's treatment illustrates the interpenetration between character construction and the style of the conversation. It is impossible to tell what came first—Ofra's externalizing tendency and fighting disposition, or the epic dialogue with its focus upon combat and acceptance.)

3

PLOTS

When we speak of a client's narrative or the therapeutic narrative that we hope will replace it, what exactly are we referring to? The story of the client's life? The recurrent script of the client's problem? Or, perhaps, the story of the evolving therapeutic relationship? These interconnected narratives all play a role in the resolution (or perpetuation) of the client's difficulties. Thus, the client's new life-narrative, problem-narrative, and therapy-narrative develop jointly. At the end of a successful treatment, the client is possessed not only of a better account of his life, but also of a new script of problematic situations and of a positive narrative about the therapy. The three are mutually supportive. They reflect and bolster each other, so much so, that they can hardly be teased apart. For simplicity's sake, we shall refer to the blend of the three that develops in therapy as *the therapeutic narrative*.

The therapeutic narrative, like a fictional one, must attract, grip, and satisfy. Early dropout from therapy may be not unlike dropping a book after a few pages: openings are therefore crucial. Once captured, the client's attention and involvement must be kept at a high pitch; the promise of the beginning must unfold into a rewarding action. Later on, the odds and ends must be tied together, for nothing spoils a story more than a bad ending. There are further constraints on the therapeutic narrative beyond those of the fictional one. The client must participate actively in its creation and must identify with it, if the therapy is to have any effect. A tall order it might seem for a therapist of flesh and blood! Fortunately, as Bruner (1986, 1990) has persuasively argued, we are born storymakers. We construe every event, however minimal and fragmentary, into a story. Each and every session and each and every therapy are storied by client and therapist alike, at the very moment of their occurrence. We cannot act otherwise. Why bother, then, to enunciate narrative principles? In fact we need the principles to patch up our natural abilities. We need them when our stories become stuck, and we need them to recognize how the client's spontaneous stories drive him into his predicament. Let us, then, resume our plot and begin at the beginning.

OPENINGS

> Once upon a time there lived in Berlin, Germany, a man called Albinus. He was rich, respectable, happy;

> one day he abandoned his wife for the sake of a youthful mistress. He loved; he was not loved; and his life ended in disaster. This is the whole of the story and we might have left it at that had there not been profit and pleasure in the telling; and although there is plenty of space on a gravestone to contain, bound in moss, the abridged version of a man's life, detail is always welcome.

Thus begins Vladimir Nabokov's (1961), *Laughter in The Dark.* No opening could be quicker. Or are we already at the conclusion? Therapeutic openings, in contrast, are often very slow and badly out of step with the client's sense of urgency. We believe this is the reason for many a dropout. The therapist patiently assesses the situation, collects data and develops a diagnosis but, all the while, the client's house is on fire.

One of the great masters of the quick therapeutic opening is, surprisingly, a psychoanalyst. James Mann (1973), the father of time-limited psychodynamic therapy, has developed a formula for defining the treatment's central issue which, delivered at the end of the first session, engages the client quickly and deeply in the therapeutic process. The formula is an empathic narration of the client's life as an enduring clash between her major life-wish and a frustrating reality. For example: "You have always wished for acceptance and closeness. You have invested endless effort in making this wish come true. Still, you feel and have always felt the constant threat of estrangement and rejection." The therapist offers this formula as the possible central theme for a therapy that will last for precisely twelve sessions.

Mann's blitz-opening awakens contrary emotions that persist throughout the therapy: hope and positive involvement, on the one hand, and anxiety over the twelve-session limit, on the other. The therapy thus embodies in its structure the very polarity (between hopeful desire and frustrating reality) that constitute the central issue. Like an operatic overture, Mann's opening allows a glimpse of the whole action.

Other therapeutic openings also foreshadow, if less elegantly, the shape of the treatment. Take the classical instructions at the opening of an orthodox psychoanalysis, for instance. The client can only expect the development of a labyrinthine plot with endless dark passages, trapdoors, and turning points. Or the opening to a behavioral exposure treatment: the client must brace herself for the coming trials or give up the enterprise from the start. Or the prologue to an experiential encounter group in which participants are asked to hold each other's hands and close their eyes. All of these prime the client about what is to come. The narratives that are entered through such different portals must be very different, indeed.

Drugs and the Couple[1]

> Silvia, a 25-year old pharmacy student, came to therapy with a double request: she wanted to maintain and improve her relationship with Mario, a writer who had been addicted to opiates for many years, and she wanted also, to help him (and herself) to kick the habit. She constantly encouraged him to stop smoking and had

1. This case appears also in Omer (1995).

nursed him through his withdrawal attempts. Lately, however, she found herself smoking with him more and more frequently.

Mario had already wasted most of his father's inheritance on drugs. He had not written for years and his life now consisted mainly of smoking, trying to stop about once every two months, and liquidating more and more of his assets to pay for his habit. Silvia was in love and would not even consider leaving him. She would not, however, agree to have children before they were both clean. Lately, her studies and her work had begun to suffer from her life-style with Mario and only luck had saved her from failing all her exams. Her father, who was paying for the therapy, had told her peremptorily that if she did not leave her junkie friend she would become a junkie herself (*drug-addict* was a taboo word with Silvia and Mario, to say nothing of *junkie*). She was afraid for her future, but hated her father for riding roughshod over her hopes and feelings. She felt that if she gave in to him, he would wipe her out as an individual as he had done with her mother and sister.

After seeing Mario, the therapist came to view things very much like Silvia's father. Mario seemed to be completely unaware of his condition. He denied that he had a serious drug problem and he rejected all offers of help, telling the therapist that he was sure he could quit on his own. All he needed was a trip abroad dedicated to that purpose (he had already had several). He felt bad that Silvia was smoking, but he was sure things would turn out well, since he was going to stop, anyway.

The therapist's view of the situation, which he had so far succeeded in keeping to himself, turned him into a potential proxy for the father, precluding the development of a therapeutic alliance. The therapist believed that without Mario, Silvia would stop, as she could abstain from drugs whenever Mario was away. However, when she was with Mario she felt unable to abstain. After two sessions (one with Silvia and one with Mario), the situation seemed already so unpromising that the therapist decided to bring the case to a group consultation which I supervised.

The therapist (and initially also the group) viewed the problem as an ineluctable chain of dependence; Mario was addicted to drugs and Silvia was addicted to Mario. So long as the chain hung together, Silvia would sink deeper into drugs. Mario and drugs came together or not at all. This description of the problem raised impossible odds for the therapeutic relationship. The therapist would actually be saying: It is either I or Mario. To make the prospects for therapy even bleaker, this was also the view of Silvia's father. After a brainstorming session that took more than two hours, a new perspective emerged.

(The constraints upon the therapy's opening and plot were quite formidable: (1.) the option of Silvia's relationship with Mario had to be kept alive; (2.) Silvia's suspicions that the therapist was her father's proxy had to be allayed; and (3.) Silvia's involvement with drugs had to be stopped before it became too late. No wonder it took more than two hours for the group to devise an opening to launch the therapy. The task was like solving a whodunit, with the difference that the solution had to answer to the story's beginning instead of its ending.)

"You have three legitimate goals. First, you want to give your relationship with Mario a real chance. Second, you want to have a full life and not the shred of one that drugs would leave to you. Third, you don't want to be crushed by your father's authority. The big question, is: Can these goals be pursued together? Your father doesn't think so. I gather from your despair, that at least at times, you don't think so, too. And, to tell you the truth, I was also skeptical. However, I asked for a professional consultation to get help with your problem and I am now much encouraged.

"I understood that for your relationship with Mario to develop it is vital that drugs stop being the bond between you. The drug is the bond between you, both when you smoke together and when you help Mario to withdraw. In both cases you two communicate through the drug and are united by the drug. Thus, if you encourage Mario to stop you are feeding the drug-bond. If you don't go to the university or to work when he tries to withdraw, you are feeding the drug-bond. If you argue with him about the drug, you are feeding the drug-bond. If you discuss the influence of the drug on your family plans, you are feeding the drug-bond. Of course, when you smoke together, when you reminisce together about drug experiences, when you have drug-sex, you are feeding the drug-bond. Your life with Mario will only have a real chance when the drug-bond will cease to exist. Then, you may have a Silvia–Mario bond, instead. But how can you achieve this? Should you turn your back on him when he is enduring the pains of withdrawal? I think you should then act as if he were suffering from a bad case of influenza. If he had the flu, would you go to work? Sure you would. You might phone him from work or from the university. You might bring him something to eat. You might prepare him some hot soup. I think this would be the best possible help whenever he attempts to withdraw. Should you not encourage him when he plans to withdraw? I think you shouldn't. When you encourage him, you do not help him. On the contrary, you hurt your relationship. I think you should resign yourself to the fact that Mario can only stop without your help. With your help, he would rather smoke. If you refuse to play the savior, he may in the end save himself, maybe six months from now, maybe a year. You cannot help him directly. You can only build a Silvia–Mario bond instead of the drug-bond.

"In dissolving the drug-bond in favor of a Silvia–Mario bond, you will also be giving yourself the chance for a fuller life. You will go back to work and you will start to study again. Each day you study, you will be dissolving the drug-bond. Each day you go to work, you will be building the Silvia–Mario bond. In leaving him alone and coming back to him in the evening, you will be giving yourself a chance and giving you both a chance.

"As for the third goal: when you feed the drug-bond, you prove your father right; when you build a Silvia–Mario bond instead, you prove him wrong. You don't have to tell him about this. If you tell him that you are now fully back at school and work, he will probably pooh-pooh it. But it is the fact, not the telling, that matters. You will then be acting out of your own need and not out of deference or rebellion."

The therapist later described how, as he delivered the message to Silvia, he grew progressively involved in the emerging narrative. Silvia recognized herself in the therapist's empathic narrative and the therapeutic alliance was on. The ensuing treatment had to face tremendous challenges, for the drug-bond fought back. After six-months of treatment and many setbacks, Silvia told the therapist she wanted to quit therapy. The therapist felt that she had decided in favor of the drug and did not want him to disturb her any longer. Three months later, however, she called to tell him that, encouraged by the therapy, she had joined a withdrawal program. She had already decided to do so when she left therapy, but had decided not to tell him out of fear that she would fail again. She had been clean for the last three months and did not even dream of going back to drugs. She was still with Mario who still smoked. He had also given the program a try after Silvia's withdrawal, but with no success. Silvia was studying and working and felt she had begun to live again.

(The plot turned out as we had forseen it in the opening. Silvia was clean and Mario smoked. The drug-bond had been dissolved but the Sylvia–Mario bond had remained.)

PERIPETEIA (REVERSAL)

The Greeks listed three major ways of plot development: *peripeteia* (reversal), *agon* (contest), and *crisis*. Aristotle viewed *peripeteia* as the very heart of drama. Thus, Oedipus, in searching for the murderer of the previous king, discovers that he is the criminal he is looking for. The whole play turns on this axis.

Peripeteia is no less crucial in psychotherapy, which, by definition, aims at transformation. Our expectations of reversal in therapy, however, are not confined to those that take place within the client. We expect to witness *peripeteia* in the treatment itself. We hope constantly for the moment of breakthrough, the sudden eruption of lost memories, the surprising turn of events. At heart, we all wish for the therapy to climax in a big surprise.

Although most treatments do not expressly plan for reversals, some do. Consider, for example, the typical stages of a treatment by hypnotic abreaction: (1.) the client's life-path is blocked and his condition is attributed to repressed memories; (2.) hypnosis and abreaction are induced; and (3.) the client starts on a new path. This sequence follows closely the three stages of cultural rites of passage: (1.) a symbolic representation of the old state that is to be abandoned; (2.) an intermediate stage characterized by suspension of ordinary rules and modes of experiencing; and (3.) a symbolic rebirth into the new state (van Gennep 1960).

The most challenging and rewarding *peripeteias* are probably those that follow from the development of therapeutic impasse. Impasse situations show with great clarity the narrative odds against which the therapy labors. Often, what looks like a client's resistance turns out to be a hidden narrative, clamoring for recognition. The shift from the manifest to the hidden narrative will then constitute a *peripeteia*. Thus, as in a mystery novel the heroine (and the reader) is at times required to retrace her steps, go back to the start, and find out that the the story is quite different from what it seemed.

A Problem of Sexual Orientation

John was 38, single, and homosexual. He dreamed of building himself a family and asked one of the authors whether he could be helped to change his sexual orientation. He had never had coital sex with a woman. A few unsuccessful experiences in his early youth had convinced him to stop trying. Sometimes however, he enjoyed having a woman as a third partner, when he was with another man.

Except for his sexual problem, John viewed himself, justifiably, as a successful person. He was a highly regarded manager in a big industrial firm and many people came to him for advice on practical as well as personal matters. His homosexuality, however, was a guarded and, for him, shameful secret. He was so disgusted with his homosexuality that he sometimes chose to abstain from sex. He would rather masturbate with the help of hazy fantasies of group sex. Even in fantasy, however, he would not touch a woman. I thought that his age, his long years as a homosexual, his total inexperience with women, and his aversion to approach them even in fantasy suggested a very poor prospect for a change in sexual orientation. John was also skeptical but felt he had to try. I agreed, therefore, even if only to help him eventually better to accept his inclinations. I proposed that we should make use of his usual sex fantasies: he would imagine himself having group sex and as orgasm approached he would gradually bring himself into closer contact with the women in the fantasy. I explained to him that this might lead to a reconditioning of his erotic responses. He found the idea very reasonable.

John also asked for my help in trying to realize an old dream of his; he wanted to build a cabin on a hill and live in it. Unoccupied hills are hard to find in Israel and building regulations are strict. The cost of this dream seemed prohibitive for, in spite of his good salary, John had saved little in past years. His cabin dream seemed, therefore, quite far-fetched, but still, he kept harping on it. Gradually, a flimsy possibility appeared on the horizon. John would have to persuade a long list of functionaries, overcome myriad obstacles, and invest himself body and soul in the project. The dream made psychological sense, however. It was not only that he wanted to live close to nature, but the cabin on the hill would be a positive, concrete manifestation of John's distinctiveness. He wanted a personal cabin on a hill in a society in which there were no personal cabins on hills. In pursuing such a peculiar goal, he would manifest (and perhaps grow to accept) his peculiarities. I supported him.

The cabin on the hill turned out to be a more practical idea than the reconditioning therapy. After six months of bureaucratic and financial somersaults, he began to build the cabin with his own hands. The sexual project, however, was floundering. It turned out that spelling out John's hazy fantasies into detailed scenes prevented his arousal altogether. This strange homosexual seemed to dislike men as well! Something seemed wrong with the therapeutic story. I decided to begin, once again, from the beginning.

(This was a critical juncture: the therapist might have decided together with John that the sexual therapy had proved ineffective, as both had suspected it would. However, he chose to focus on the one piece in the puzzle that didn't fit: John's lack of arousal in sexual fantasies with males and females alike. The therapist had no idea where this negative clue might be leading.)

John told me once again how, at the age of 18, he had tried and failed to have sex with women. He had told it all before, and we had the feeling that we were wasting time. However, the story now took a different turn. John's first sexual experience had ended in premature ejaculation. He decided to get professional help and found a professor who advertised himself in the Yellow Pages as a specialist in sexual disorders. He made an appointment. The professor listened to him carefully and asked many questions. At the end of the interview he told John that the reason behind his failure was that he was a latent homosexual; women were a threat for him. Homosexuality, the professor added, was no shame; he should accept his inclinations instead of trying to fight against them. John was deeply shaken. In the next few months he tried repeatedly but unavailingly to have sex with women. Crestfallen, he returned to the professor who told him that he now had obtained the final proof that women were not for him. John should now try to have sex with men as a critical experiment that would show him the difference. John tried and functioned, technically at least. He had been scientifically proved to be a homosexual.

I felt the situation called for an official reversal of the professor's verdict. I told John that the six months we had spent in our failed attempt at reconditioning suggested that he was a very strange homosexual. In my whole career and in all the textbooks I had read, I had never met with a homosexual less attracted to men. This new evidence justified us in reopening his case. I chose this legal-scientific terminology, because the professor's influence over John devolved upon his scientific arguments.

I told John that even if the professor had been right in diagnosing a homosexual tendency, this might well have been a normal phenomenon for an adolescent. I showed John quotes from heavy textbooks on the subject of normative bisexuality in adolescence. Maybe John had never really been a latent homosexual. Perhaps what he had been suffering from all these years was latent heterosexuality! This suppressed inclination might explain why he was not attracted to men. The new hypothesis deserved to be tested with the same thoroughness as the one on latent homosexuality. The professor's assumption that John's premature ejaculation had been caused by latent homosexuality was, to say the least, unparsimonious. The simplest way to account for John's adolescent sexual dysfunction was that it was due to anxiety.

I inquired about the professor and, as luck would have it, there had been complaints about him to the Ministry of Health. There were also doubts about his academic credentials. I told John of my findings, and that the ministry would be very glad to have a written deposition from him. Instead of chasing after old ghosts, however, John chose to focus on the present. I agreed, particularly since I felt that the work of discreditation had already achieved its goal.

(The development of the new plot was made possible by a retelling of the once-told story from the vantage point of the clue that didn't fit. The positive side of the therapeutic peripeteia turned upon the quaint expression "latent heterosexuality." This new diagnostic label made for a completely new direction in the evolving story.)

I told John that we might assume that he was suffering at present not only from the insecurity of a typical adolescent, but also from the consequences of prolonged disuse. He had no experience whatsoever of intimacy with women. We would have to build, patiently, the foundations for the new experiment. On his side John had the wisdom of maturity, for unlike a youngster, he knew that he did not have to succeed all at once. The goal might seem unattainable without being so; the cabin was the proof. We started on a program of graded courtship training.

John began to spend time with women and became personally close to them. He was, however, to avoid for the moment, all physical intimacy. Under these safe conditions he could check whether he felt any attraction. He did. However, once he tried to become more intimate, he found that the women he chose were not interested. We were puzzled, for John is an attractive man. It slowly transpired that he was choosing the wrong partners. As if he still were an adolescent, he was trying to date very young women, for he said that only very young women attracted him. We discussed at length whether attraction was an absolute given or something that might slowly ripen. For instance, he had not known for years that he was attracted to women. Now, he knew he was. I proposed that the issue of attraction to mature women should also be decided experimentally. John liked the idea.

(The new reversed plot builds on the elements of the discarded one. The use of experiments to decide on John's inclinations was thus a theme taken up from John's previous narrative. Each new experiment had the advantage of refuting anew the professor's predictions. This use of the professor as a foil is similar to the well-known procedure in detective novels of having a stupid policeman make all the wrong guesses, thus giving salience to the smart detective's eventual elucidation.)

In a few months, John had developed a close relationship with a divorced woman. She invited him to visit her and offered to massage him when he complained of shoulder pains. I encouraged him to accept the invitation and to play close attention to any erotic feelings that might emerge. This relationship, which gradually turned into a fully sexual one, lasted for a few months. After that John became personally and sexually intimate with a couple of other women. Gradually feeling more secure he left the therapy. A year later he returned with a woman he wanted to marry; they had some initial sexual difficulties that I helped them overcome. They were married, have two daughters, and are living in the cabin on the hill.

AGON (CONTEST)

Agon is the clash between protagonist and antagonist, hero and villain, or thesis and antithesis, at the center of the action. White and Epston (1990) fathered the idea of setting *agon* at the very center of psychotherapy. The first therapeutic task, in their view, is the construal of the problem as the treatment's villain, against which the client's forces are mobilized. A good villain, however, is hard to find; there are many constraints that should be kept in mind regarding this fact. Thus, the villain should not be some uneradicable trait of the client's; or be so defined as to involve the client in irredeemable clashes with important others; or give rise to a spurious belief in conspiracies.

Sometimes, what is needed is a partialization of the antagonist; instead of viewing him as wholly bad, we may help the client to winnow the villainous chaff from the virtuous wheat. For example, perfectionist clients often feel persecuted by an inner critical voice. The difficulty in treating such clients often stems from the fact that they may react badly to attempts to silence this critical voice, for they feel that this voice also represents what is best within them. The therapist might then argue, for instance, that the voice's goals are positive but its methods flawed; or, that the voice may have played a vital role in the past, but that it has grown anachronistic in the present; or, that the voice is right in certain areas, but wrong in others. Split villains with a positive side, if empathically narrated, can make for rich narrative arguments.

At other times, the difficulty is that one's enemy may be another's friend. Or that a family may be divided precisely upon the definition of the villain. The construction of a common, unifying enemy may then be quite a therapeutic challenge.

Rashomon of Abuse

Gali arrived in therapy with a complaint of text-anxiety. She was 16 and usually a good pupil. Lately however, every new exam had become an ordeal for the whole family. Gali would become very tense in the days before the exam, make anxious phone calls to her classmates and teachers, scream at those around her and throw things about. On two occasions, she had even slashed herself (luckily not deeply) on the arms and wrists.

Gali attributed the anxiety to her father's harsh scholastic demands from her in the past. He would force her to rewrite all of her homework from the start if he found one mistake in it. He would keep her at her desk until she could answer any question he might pose. On the smallest pretext he would rave, threaten and, at times, resort to real blows. Unexpectedly, two years ago he had ended his involvement with Gali's studies. Far from feeling relieved, however, Gali asked her mother to take over the father's role and make sure that she prepared herself thoroughly for her exams. Exam times became a veritable quarantine. Gali, although she had asked for it, would end up so tense that an explosion was sure to occur.

The mother viewed things differently. She had suffered badly from test-anxiety herself, to the point of being unable to attend college. She feared that the problem might be genetic and that Gali was destined to suffer from the same handicaps as she did. The father, on his side, thought that the whole thing was just a manipulation of Gali's, an excuse for her failings, and an attention-getting device. One either prepared for one's exams or not, and that was it. The mother was playing into Gali's hands by making such a fuss about the problem. His wife, he said, had the habit of turning the slightest problems into major catastrophes. Thus, not a week went by without her turning a small physical discomfort into a major illness. *Rashomon:* three people, three stories.

A worse disagreement had to do with another of Gali's problems. During the Gulf War two years ago, she had been unable to enter the shelter. She told her parents that she could not abide closed spaces (this was news to them). When challenged she said that there were other vital things they did not know about her. After considerable prodding, a sad story emerged; at the age of 7, she had been repeatedly abused by a babysitter. The boy, who was about 15 at the time, would shut himself in the bathroom with her, strip her, and rub his penis against her vagina. When she threatened to tell her parents, he beat her up. The abuse continued for months until the family moved to another town.

The father reacted to the disclosure with pain and anger against the perpetrator. He would find him and bring him to trial. Gali dissuaded him; there were no proofs and the whole thing would only reopen her wounds. Little by little, the parents, especially the father, came to doubt the veracity of the story. Gali had sexual relations with her boyfriend, seemingly without any problems. She had felt free to ask her parents for contraceptives. The parents wondered how, after having been repeatedly abused as a child, she could have grown so open and free about sex. There were additional reasons for their skepticism. Recently, they had been startled from their siesta by Gali's screams. They ran to her room and found her in tears and her 15-year-old brother sulking. When questioned, Gali refused to talk and the brother said she was crazy. The father pressured him to say what had happened, but to no avail. Later in the day, Gali's boyfriend called the mother and told her that Gali's brother, presuming that she was asleep, had touched her intimately. (On former occasions, the boyfriend had assumed the role of Gali's spokesperson before the family.) Gali had told him that this had been going on for a whole month. She had been paralyzed with shock, but she now decided that things had gone too far. The brother was (at least apparently) totally stunned by the accusation. The father thought it no longer wise to pretend he believed Gali's fantasies and said that he was sure that not only this, but also the old abuse story, was all baloney. Gali retorted that this only proved how useless it was to expect any help from her parents. They would only believe her if she died.

Gali's credibility was a major issue also in other areas. For instance, she complained of pains in her wrist, which disturbed her badly in exams, as well as in other situations. The father did not believe her and the mother was in doubt. She took Gali to a specialist who offered to perform a small operation on the wrist. For the mother this was a test. If Gali agreed to undergo the operation it would mean her complaints were genuine. Gali agreed, was operated on, and the hand became functional. It is hard to say, however, whether this was proof of her truthfulness rather than of her determination. At all events, the stakes in the credibility game were obviously rising to a dangerous height.

At the end of the fifth session, the father expressed his desire for a professional summary of the case. Each family member expected his own view to be vindicated. The therapist was in a bind. On one hand, even if Gali sometimes confabulated, the very tendency to confabulate might have originated with the first trauma. Her explosive reactions, fear of enclosed spaces, and tendency to panic made the traumatic hypothesis tenable. To cast doubt on the reality of her charges would then be doubly traumatizing. On the other hand, endorsing Gali's claims would alienate her father and cast grave and possibly unjustified aspersions upon Gali's brother. The therapist also felt it was very difficult to avoid taking any stand on the matters under discussion for even if she kept her opinions to herself, the family would try to read them between the lines. The therapeutic alliance would then be at the mercy of these readings.

The therapist, well versed in White and Epston's

(1990) approach, had tried in vain to find a personalized version of the problem that might unite the family in a common front. Thus, *test anxiety* was an acceptable antagonist for mother and daughter, but meaningless for father; it had the further disadvantage of leaving the abuse story untouched. *Explosiveness* might seem a common problem of Gali's and father's but, rather than unifying them it deepened their dissension, because each blamed the other for all their troubles. *Trauma* or *abuse* were unacceptable to father. *Exaggeration* or *hysteria* were unacceptable to Gali. At this juncture, the perplexed therapist brought the case to a consultation group supervised by one of the authors. The group attempted to define an antagonist that might mobilize and unify the family, thus neutralizing its inner conflicts.

(The difficulty in finding a common antagonist reflects the fragmentation of reality in the family. Gali's version was completely disqualified by the father. The mother accepted some of Gali's complaints, such as test-anxiety, but rejected others, such as the accusations against the brother. The parents' versions on the other hand were decried by Gali as attesting to their willful blindness. Between the brother and Gali, the situation was even worse: the choice devolved between his being incestuous or her being insane. A workable solution should transform these competing plots into one acceptable whodunit.)

The task was hard and it took more than three hours to complete. The following message, which was delivered in three written copies to father, mother, and Gali, is the result of this joint work:

"In the beginning, I thought we were dealing only with a problem of test-anxiety. That was, however, only the tip of the iceberg. There were also Gali's outbursts and suicide attempts to be taken into account. More was to come: grave suspicions of prolonged sexual abuse in Gali's childhood, Gali's accusations against you, parents, of willful blindness toward her and, now, the chilling story about Gali's brother. The family seems haunted by an expanding bubble of horrors. Paradoxically, the damage seems to become even worse by the very fact that we cannot say whether the cause of the horrors is true or imaginary.

"This presence that haunts you all without appearing in the open is like a *dybbuk*. But what is a *dybbuk*? It is precisely a being who is only half real. It can never be clearly seen, defined, or agreed upon. It arouses terror in its victims and skepticism in those who can't feel it. It feeds on the paralysis caused by doubt. You, Gali, suffer like the victim of a *dybbuk*. Thus, when bad things start to happen to you, you become paralyzed. You wait passively, expecting the evil to disappear, but it grows instead. In the end, you break into a panic, an attack against yourself, or a spate of awful accusations. You suffer doubly—from the problem itself and from the disbelief of others. This is the typical fate of a *dybbuk* victim: to suffer without confirmation; to accuse without proof; to feel the horror and to be plagued by doubt. You, mother, also suffer from *dybbuk*-like experiences. You feel overwhelmed at times by bodily anxieties that suddenly dissolve as if they were only imaginary. You are oppressed by fears for Gali but you cannot ferret out their cause. Even test-anxiety, which you have also experienced, is denied by your husband. You, father, are not a *dybbuk* victim but part of the *dybbuk's* supporting cast. *Dybbuks* require skeptics and you play the role to perfection. You are a *dybbuk* feeder. You can see for yourself that the more you deny your daughter's or your wife's problems, the more they grow. In denying the reality of test-anxiety, you feed it. In denying the legitimacy of your wife's anguish, you augment it. In dismissing Gali's complaints, you increase her indignant fervor. You expect that Gali will finally confess that nothing ever happened and that all her complaints were lies. She will do nothing of the kind. Nothing like this ever happens to someone who suffers from horrors. No *dybbuk* in history ever confessed to its nonexistence. The family *dybbuk* has an additional assistant: Gali's boyfriend. *Dybbuks* always search for spokespersons or for people who understand their language. Whenever the *dybbuk* oppresses Gali and she is too paralyzed to speak, you may trust her boyfriend to appear and lend the *dybbuk* his voice. Passivity, skepticism, and the presence of a helpful interpreter create the ideal conditions for a *dybbuk*.

"The question is whether the family can defeat the *dybbuk*, rather than to go on feeding him. Each of you has a role to play, for each contributes to the *dybbuk's* maintenance. You, Gali, contribute by your passivity. Whenever you refrain from acting or reacting in a determined way, you are relinquishing control to the *dybbuk*. For instance, in the story involving your brother, whose reality we can never really know, you waited and waited. You even pretended to be asleep. When, eventually you did react, it was too late; you were already completely in the *dybbuk's* grip. You also wait passively whenever your mother quarantines you at exam times. And you passively allow your boyfriend to lend the *dybbuk* his voice. You must learn to talk for yourself, to take command over your body, and to prepare on your own for your exams. In delegating all these functions to others, you invite the *dybbuk* in. You, father, play into the *dybbuk's* hands by your militant skepticism. You think you are being reasonable and helpful, but you are not. You could help Gali by quitting the skeptic's role and by not allowing quarantines, which are a veritable hothouse for *dybbuks*. You, mother, contribute to the *dybbuk* by dealing with Gali as if she were the perpetuator of your fate. *Dybbuks* relish nothing more than the belief in a good family curse. However, Gali is neither the heir to your problem nor the carrier of your curse. She has her own problems, her own challenges, and her own fate to grapple with."

The only one to react in the session was Gali. In an apparently unrelated manner, she told her parents that she understood from the message that her therapy had ended and their therapy was about to begin. She said she would decide by herself whether to come to the next session. She decided not to and the parents arrived alone. A series of sessions focusing on effective parenting ensued. Gali's outbursts ceased. She spoke no more of rape and abuse. She was left to handle her exams by herself. This much exorcism seemed to have been accomplished.

CRISIS

Crises are moments of truth in the development of plot: issues come to a head, postponement is no longer viable, the drama reaches a pitch. The Rubicon is there. Caesar may cross it or not but if he doesn't there is no story and no Caesar. Crises are no less crucial for the psychotherapist than for the novelist or dramatist. Indeed, both clients and therapists will often view a therapy without at least one crisis as a shabby product. The clinical and empirical writings on therapeutic impact confirm this judgment. The absence of high dramatic points makes for a therapy that is less engaging, less memorable, and less effective (Omer 1987, 1990, 1992; Omer et al. 1992; Omer et al. 1993).

Mostly, therapists do not create crises but exploit those that they find ready made. It was one of Freud's most influential ideas to turn the relational crises between therapist and client into therapeutic assets. What he termed the transference neurosis may thus be viewed as a natural crisis in the therapeutic relation that if well handled can be turned into the treatment's very fulcrum. Recently this idea has become central also for nonanalytic psychotherapies. Thus, Safran (1993) has proposed an approach to relational ruptures in experiential therapy by which the crises between therapist and client are developed into propitious moments of change. A similar position has developed among the proponents of the crisis intervention approach, who see a crisis not merely as a fire to be extinguished, but as an invaluable opportunity for change.

From the point of view of plot and drama, climaxes and crises are similar. Both come to epitomize the whole therapy or summarize a therapeutic stage. Sometimes, the climax is simply a crisis made good. At other times, however, it is a purely positive moment where a breakthrough is achieved or an exceptionally warm feeling experienced. The eruption of positive feelings demands from the therapist as much narrative skill as that of negative ones. In both cases the emotions must be channeled so as to become the watershed of the developing plot.

Like novels, however, therapeutic narratives can be frittered away in too many crises. We all know of treatments that flounder from crisis to crisis, leading only to exhaustion. It may then be the therapist's challenge to turn the rare quiet moment, the silent eye of the hurricane into the heart of the therapeutic narrative. It is, thus, not the amount of noise *per se* that determines an event as the narrative's turning point. Rather, it is the event's standing out from the old repetitive narrative as an extraneous growth. These qualities turn unique events into the seeds of new stories.

Cancer and Chaos

> Mira, a 50-year-old woman who worked as a volunteer in an oncological ward, phoned the therapist who was also the ward's psychologist, asking for a few words with her. They made an appointment for a few days ahead. Ten minutes after the phone call, Mira's husband, Dov, called the therapist asking for an emergency session for the two of them. The therapist agreed to see them immediately.
>
> Dov told the therapist that in the course of the last month Mira had traveled twice to another town and spent the night at a hotel without telling anyone about her plans or whereabouts. Mira said she had boarded the bus by mistake and replied evasively when questioned about these episodes. Dov said that Mira had probably not been conscious of what had happened to her and that there had been other recent events when she had been uncharacteristically forgetful. For instance, though she had always kept the family's budget strictly in hand, she had lately forgotten to pay a whole set of bills. These and other atypical memory lapses had led

Dov and Mira's elder daughter (a social worker) to suspect that Mira might be suffering from dissociative disorder.

There were other big reasons for worry. Mira had cancer, and the disease had first shown itself fifteen years earlier. Mira had cooperated with all treatments but lately had not shown up for a scheduled operation and had abruptly stopped taking all her medications. Dov had always detached himself from everything that concerned Mira's illness, saying that he would panic if he were to come near a hospital. Apparently, Mira was satisfied with Dov's attitude; she never complained and she also kept her children from helping her. She had done everything on her own, to the point of going alone to her operations and refusing all visits when she was in the hospital.

Dov knew next to nothing about Mira's medical condition. He had never gone with her to a single appointment with a physician. Actually in this respect Dov was a typical representative of his family, for all the problems of the household and with all family members had always been Mira's sole responsibility. Dov had a very busy schedule as the head of a research project and it had been agreed between them that all daily concerns fell within Mira's province.

In spite of Dov's detachment, the spouses held their relationship to have been excellent in the past. In the last two years, however, Mira suspected that Dov was having an affair with a research assistant. Dov denied that the relationship was sexual but Mira had no doubts. A few weeks previously she had even made an unannounced visit to her rival's home. She had been disgusted by the way the house was kept and wondered how Dov could be intimate with such a dirty woman.

The session was veering from crisis to crisis. After the fugues, the cancer, and the infidelity, came the problems with the daughters. The elder had recently canceled her wedding on its very eve. Mira, who had hoped to live to see her daughter's family life launched, was disappointed and worried. The younger daughter was in trouble, too. Always a brilliant student, she had recently dropped out of college. Mira felt she could not even die in peace.

Toward the end of the session, Dov surprised Mira by asking to go with her to the oncologist, so that they might review her condition together. Mira refused; her illness was her own business. She also wanted the therapy to be individual. Well trained in leaving all troubled fields to Mira, Dov agreed. The therapist, however, refused to make any decision before receiving a neurologist's opinion on Mira's memory lapses and their possible relationship to her illness.

The neurologist uncovered a long-standing history of epilepsy. Mira had been born with a brain tumor and had survived its removal against all expectations. As a result, however, she had suffered all through her childhood and youth from epileptic seizures that were only partially controlled by anti-convulsants. The seizures disappeared in early adulthood and did not return when Mira stopped taking the medication during her first pregnancy. For many years, Mira remained unmedicated and asymptomatic. Recently, however, there had been signs that the epilepsy had returned. The psychiatrist sent Mira for an EEG that revealed highly abnormal focal activity, and a CT-scan that found no brain metastases. Mira was put again on anti-convulsants.

The therapist then agreed to Mira's request for a number of individual sessions. During their meetings Mira talked mostly about Dov's dirty affair. Except for that, nothing seemed to bother her. At home, too, she started complaining more and more about Dov's infidelity. She could not understand why he had so soiled their lifelong friendship. To appease her anger and be able to stay with her more, Dov decided to resign as head of the research project and take a home sabbatical. Mira, however, would not let him help her. She was resentful over all the years he had left her alone with the illness and would punish him by not letting him in at this stage.

When she had talked her fill about the affair, Mira told the therapist how she had grown up under the shadow of death. She had not been expected to survive for long and had actually lived all her youth on borrowed time. She felt very much alive whenever she succeeded in becoming autonomous in any field and taking things under her sole control. From very early youth she had taken pride in supporting herself financially (although her parents had been willing to help her). She went to the university and could have had an academic career, but to everyone's surprise she married, became pregnant, and chose to dedicate herself to her family. Her care for her husband and daughters bordered on outright spoiling: Dov and the girls could not cook an egg.

After a few sessions with Mira, the therapist had one with Dov. In contrast to Mira, Dov had been reared from earliest childhood as a genius who should not waste his time with the trivia of daily life. Others should care for him: first his parents, and later on Mira, who, with her desire to be in control, found the role much to her liking. Recently when Mira had been confined to bed, the youngest daughter had tried to help in the kitchen. Mira soon chased the girl from her domain. She simply could not stop being in charge.

Overwhelmed with the family's multiple emergencies, the therapist came for a consultation. She felt that Mira and Dov were flooding her. The group discussion initially echoed the therapist's predicament, jumping disconnectedly from problem to problem. But the group converged on the issue of Mira's inability to accept help. Her overzealous self-reliance and need to maintain control seemed to be paralyzing the family. Any attempt by Dov and their daughters to take an active part in managing the household would, in Mira's present condition, signal her that she was being written off. In the family dictionary, any helpfulness shown by Dov or the girls would be read as despair about Mira's prospects.

The group considered the possibility of working with Mira to make her more amenable to accepting help, but the therapist felt that time was too short for such a course. The psychological emergency would have to be addressed within the time boundaries of the medical one. Furthermore, the issues of Dov's putative infidelity and his record of noninvolvement with Mira's illness would also have to be addressed. A tall order for a few sessions!

(Like the reader of a novel who thumbs through the remaining pages of the book, fearing there are too few to allow for a resolution of the story's multiple intrigues, the therapist felt that unless the different strands were pulled together at once, the treatment would surely unravel.)

The following message embodies the group's attempt to bring all of the family's multiple problems under one head.

"After our joint and individual sessions, I have reached some conclusions that I must share with you. I want to begin with you, Dov. You wanted to go with Mira to an oncologist, so that you two might review her medical condition together. You were absolutely right and I believe that you must stick to that line and find a way to overrule Mira's objections. You have finally chosen to become involved. That is the right decision as a human being, a husband, and a father. Your voice must be heard. For the sake of Mira, for the sake of you both, and for the sake of the children, do not let her keep you out. To do so will be acquiescing to the destruction of your lifelong friendship. You cannot allow your anxiety or your habits to prevent you from becoming Mira's companion in her hardest hours. On the contrary, you must pick up the challenge and revoke the unacceptable edict under which you grew up and that made you unfit for partaking of human troubles. Even if Mira doesn't allow you in, you have to fight your way. You have to wake up with her, eat with her, talk with her, walk with her, and convince her that you will not leave her alone.

"As for you, Mira—your life taught you not to let anyone help you. This was your protest of autonomy, your way of staying alive, despite the death sentence that had been pronounced against you. Today, however, you will be causing endless damage by not allowing Dov to help you. You will be allowing your daughters to witness the disintegration of your family. You may be avenging yourself on Dov, but at the price of all that is dearest to you. You have to let him offer reparation. You must allow him to be with you and to help take care of you. If you let him in, he will be with *you* and not with the other woman, and you will be busy with your family and not obsessing about her. You will help Dov and the girls learn to manage. You will be active with them for as long as you can. By so doing, you will also help them learn how to let you depart when the time comes. I believe that this task must be more worthy in your eyes than revenge. I am sure that you will not relinquish your responsibility, which is now to let your husband and your daughters help you."

(The message was framed in the language of crisis, without hesitancy or tentativeness. It spoke to the therapist's and the couple's sense of urgency and need for a unifying focus. It pulled the different emergencies together, opening a wide avenue for joint effort. It mobilized Mira's and Dov's feelings for each other, their need of companionship, their hope for reparation, and their common concern for the girls. It also made a powerful bid to dismantle Mira's self-defeating strategy and Dov's self-incapacitating beliefs. So much could be aimed for because of the crisis, and because the message was charged with narrative empathy.)

Dov and Mira took up the challenge. It turned out that Mira had to stop chemotherapy because of liver complications. Dov became very much involved in the treatment of the epilepsy. The fugues stopped although the motor seizures remained. Dov was fully at home and fully engaged. There was no longer talk of the other woman. Mira and Dov started to go for short trips together. Their renewed companionship and their joint consideration and care of Mira's physical problems left little need for further psychotherapy. The therapist soon reduced the frequency of the sessions. The therapy was concluded three months after the delivery of the message.

ENDINGS

A bad ending not only puts a stop to all therapeutic interventions, but is a harmful intervention in itself. An unexplained dropout, an indignant doorslam, or a phasing-out after an agonizing stalemate causes damage as well as unpleasantness. They add another failure to a chain of earlier ones. They breed distrust and stain all previous achievements.

But what counts as a good ending? Different therapies pose different requirements. The belief in one universal right ending is as groundless as the belief in the one right therapy. Therapies that are conducted in a lighthearted mode cannot end like those in which a romantic or an epic tone prevail. The right ending can be quite a peculiar affair. Alon (1985) developed an unusual variety of endings to the treatment of clients who had been diagnosed as suffering from post-traumatic stress disorder and who had been previously (often multiply) treated without success. These clients expected the therapy to start with the trauma as their previous unsuccessful therapies had done. Many of them had already become so inured to this approach, that the mere mention of the trauma brought to their eyes an expression of endless fatigue: Here we go again, they seemed to be saying. Treatment should therefore reverse the expected order; rehabilitation should come first and elaboration of the trauma, last. The dominant therapeutic message became: "You must get stronger in order to deal with the trauma." Improvement became the condition for abreaction. The client had to be, functionally, no longer a post-traumatic in order to become eligible for it. In this manner, confrontation with the trauma was turned into the treatment's rite of conclusion. The beginning became the end.

What happens, however, when therapy fails? How can it then be rightly ended? It may be an optimist's dream, but we like to think that no therapy should be abandoned as a total loss. Omer (1991) has proposed that even a treatment that ended on a very bad note may still be salvaged by a written post-scriptum that attempts to rectify the previous mistakes. It is precisely at these difficult junctures that we therapists are most in need of a richer sense of plot. We may draw encouragement in our bleak moments from Mark Twain's story *A Medieval Romance* (1870/1983). The hero, Conrad, is actually a woman who was raised from birth as a man, so as to become eligible for a dukedom. At the end of the story, Conrad can only save him- or herself from the charge of getting his or her lovely cousin pregnant (the penalty for which is death), by declaring himself to be herself (the penalty for which is death). We are very near the end of the story. There is only one paragraph left. In a statement whose grammar might be acclaimed as one of the earliest non-sexist jewels in literature, Mark Twain ties up his impossible plot:

> The truth is, I have got my hero or heroine into such a particularly close place that I do not see how I am ever going to get him or her out of it again, and therefore I will wash my hands of the whole business, and leave that person to get out the best way that offers—or else stay there. I thought it was going to be easy enough to straighten out that little difficulty, but it looks different now. [p. 56]

It is a pity that such a solution cannot be applied again and again. Or can it? Psychotherapy might perhaps be a promising ground for this piece of insight.

In the End is the Beginning

Sara was 10 and for half her life she had been in therapy. Her parents had been involved in bitter divorce proceedings since she was 5. Both underwent psychiatric examinations by order of the court and both were diagnosed as suffering from personality disorders. The court ruled that Sara must stay with the mother. The social worker in charge of the case requested that Sara be placed in therapy and the court ruled accordingly. Three years later, a higher court found the mother incapable and transferred Sara's custody to the father as the lesser of two evils. The father in the meantime had married again and had a new baby. Sara's mother was accorded visiting rights.

In spite of these untoward events, Sara seemed to be developing well: she was bright, active, and sociable and did very well at school. Still, there was reason for worry. Sara had witnessed horrible things since her earliest childhood. Her mother had repeatedly tried to commit suicide. On one occasion, 4-year old Sara had called the neighbors, on finding her mother bleeding on the floor. There had been many other shocking scenes: the mother would at times scream uncontrollably, claiming that her ex-husband was trying to drive her insane. She would then take Sara to his house, knock wildly at the door, call him and his new wife names, and fall to the ground in a swoon. More frequently, she would just stay in bed for days on end, whimpering to her daughter about her fate. In these bouts of lamentation Sara would be told, among other ugly stories, that her father chased after women every night and after abusing them put their pictures in an album that he cherished as he might a butterfly collection.

Sara expressed herself very maturely for a 5-year old and told the therapist that things were all right with her and that she did not want any help. During all her years in therapy she never changed this line. Her arguments as she grew only became more cogent. At the age of 10, she blamed the therapist, the social worker, and the judge for forcing her into therapy against her will and for not caring about the rights of children. Still, she arrived punctually. When she could not come, she would phone the therapist to tell her. In the therapy room, she agreed to play only highly structured games. She knew what the therapist was after and she would not comply. Thus, if the therapist interpreted any of her art productions, she would immediately stop her activity. Once she drew a picture of a man pointing a gun at himself. When the therapist said something about the possible significance of the drawing, Sara tore the sheet to bits and never drew in therapy again.

From the moment she passed into her father's custody, Sara refused to meet with her mother. She would run away when the mother approached. The mother appealed to the court, saying that the father was preventing her visits. From then on, the meetings with Sara took place in the social worker's office. The mother would beg Sara to talk to her and Sara would keep her mouth shut. Undaunted, the mother would ambush her on her way from school and attempt to squeeze a few words from her. Sara developed a lingering fear that the mother would appear and kept a constant watch to spot her before she came too near.

Once, in the middle of a therapy session, Sara froze, believing she had heard her mother outside. After two years of chasing and fleeing, the mother gave up and stopped forcing herself upon Sara. Sara's fears diminished and, little by little, she even agreed to communicate with the mother by phone. She used this development as a new argument to end the therapy: "You see, everything is all right! I even talk to my mother. So why do I have to come here?"

There were signs, however, that belied Sara's blitheness. Sometimes she would cry for hours because she had lost a coin or because she disliked the sound of her voice on the tape-recorder. The therapist also worried about the new family setup for Sara never mentioned her father, his wife, or the baby. When asked, she said everything was O.K. The therapist felt that Sara's attitude of rigid denial combined dangerously with the father's untrustworthiness. She feared for Sara's safety with the father; the mother's stories might after all not be wholly groundless. These were good reasons to keep Sara under watch. Still, the therapist asked herself whether the treatment was helping Sara, rather than the contrary. Forcing Sara into a relationship that she did not want was a painful replay of the previous drama with her mother. Moreover, therapy was teaching Sara how to shut herself off even more tightly; she had, for instance, learned that drawing was dangerous! Stopping the therapy, however, would diminish the chances that Sara might eventually grow more willing to examine herself and allow others into her difficulties. These doubts brought the therapist to a consultation with one of the authors.

In the course of the consultation, the inner logic of Sara's noncooperative stance became clearer. Sara lived in constant fear of her mother who was, in her eyes, the very embodiment of psychological problems. Understandably, she tried to keep as distant and distinct from her mother as she could. She did not want to be *with* her or *like* her. Her mother, not she, was the kind of person who went to therapists. Furthermore, the mother had said that therapists drive people crazy, and she was the living proof of such an assertion. To be in therapy meant that Sara was in some sense similar to her mother. Consequently, she could not agree that she had problems or needed therapy. She absolutely had to believe that her therapy was a mistake. Paradoxically, the therapy, instead of helping Sara to open up, was only making her more defensive. The more resourceful the therapist, the more tightly would Sara have to shut herself up. Stopping the therapy might perhaps free her from this bind. She would have won the battle and might then be able to unbuckle her armor.

This empathic narrative led to a reappraisal of Sara's psychological condition. Would another child with a similar behavior profile be sent to therapy? Most probably not. Ever since her life situation had stabilized, Sara's only symptoms had been her refusal to see her mother, her occasional persistent crying in frustrating situations, and her defensive stance in therapy. Socially, scholastically, and personally, Sara seemed to be doing very well.

But what about Sara's father? Was not his dubious character reason enough for therapeutic watchfulness? The new narrative line allowed us to reappraise this issue as well. The only grounds for suspicion against the father had been the mother's accusations and the psychiatric interview, which had taken place at the height of the litigation when the father could be expected to be under great stress. As far as was known, his actual behavior towards Sara was irreproachable.

For safety's sake, another consultation session was held to make sure if the therapy should indeed be terminated. A careful reassessment of the evidence returned the same verdict: not only should the therapy be concluded, but Sara should be confirmed in her belief that she had in fact, never needed any therapy. The judicial mistake was to be corrected and Sara exonerated from any possible psychotherapeutic taint. The following message was meant to serve as such a quasi-official recantation:

"I have some surprising news to give you. I thought a lot about you lately and reached the conclusion that you were right all along—you need no therapy. Since you first came to me five years ago, you have always said, 'I am O.K. What do you want from me?' As you grew up you said the same thing, but more strongly, 'It is wrong to force children to do something that they don't want and don't need.' And you said the same in words that I will never forget, 'You and that Freud of yours!' It took me a long time to understand that you were absolutely right. You are well, healthy, smart, and fun to be with.

"I want you to know that I care for you and like you very much. If ever you want my help or if you want a piece of advice, I will be happy to hear from you. And, I will not think that you need therapy. I am also writing to the court that you do not have to be in therapy and I will tell your father the same. I am sure that the way you are developing you will grow to be a marvelous woman, just as you are a marvelous girl."

Sara was struck dumb. When the therapist offered to hug her, she responded warmly. Later in the day the therapist heard from Sara's father that she had run to his office right after the session to tell him the news. She could hardly believe it and was bursting with happiness.

A couple of weeks after the final session, Sara met with the social worker (whom the mother had again asked to mediate between them) and told her with pride about the conclusion of the therapy.

(This ending invites comparison with the Milan School's procedure for the abdication of a therapeutic team [Boscolo et al. 1987]. With the Milanese, too, the decision to abdicate follows from the team's recognition that they have been playing a negative role. The abdication aims at reversing this unproductive line. In contrast to our present approach, however, the clients have no part in the therapist's decision and they are not consulted on the issue. Sometimes it is precisely because the clients have become too well-accommodated to the therapeutic team that the latter decides to stop the treatment. There is a further difference: with the Milan School, the rationale for termination is often delivered tongue-in-cheek. These differences illustrate the transition from a strategic or paradoxical approach to a narratively empathic one.[2] *In striving for narrative empathy, the therapist reaches for a position that both she and the client may endorse. The client's emotional resonance and the therapist's sense of being at one with the message are equally crucial. Thus, in the present case the empathic construal of Sara's behavior made the message fully acceptable to both parties.)*

---

2. This description applies especially to the earlier writings of the Milan School. In recent years, their position has become very close to a narratively empathic one.

4

THEMES

Although it does not figure as such in psychotherapeutic primers, thematic work is an everyday therapeutic activity. Such themes surface when (1.) a psychoanalyst reveals to the client the thematic similarity in a series of dreams; (2.) a Jungian therapist expands on a theme brought out by the client by placing it in a broader cultural context; (3.) a therapist who uses the technique of guided imagery has the client develop a series of variations on a theme; (4.) a family therapist uses circular interviewing to introduce variability into a family's thematic monolith.

If it is so common, why, then, is thematic work not acknowledged as such? Probably because therapists have usually been averse to accepting the similarities between psychotherapy and the arts. Thematic work smacks too much of literature or music for a purportedly scientific discipline. Under the new narrative dispensation, however, psychotherapy's kinship to the arts loses its negative connotation. We can, therefore, openly accept and declare that among the therapist's skills the definition and elaboration of themes figures prominently. Indeed, the similarity between psychotherapy and the arts in this respect is quite deep, for the basic forms of elaboration are similar for both. Thus, artistic or therapeutic effects are created by the same processes of playing upon thematic unity, recapitulation, variation, and contraposition.

THEMATIC UNITY

Formlessness is a threat for any kind of therapy. The need for order is so compelling as to rule out the feasibility of such psychoanalytic desiderata as free association and evenly hovering attention. Indeed, the psychoanalytic session must either become thematically organized or risk drowning in the client's stream of consciousness. In order to guarantee a modicum of order, the analyst must subject the productions of the client to a complex organizing activity, assuming, for instance, that a common theme underlies the separate details of an hour, a dream, or a set of associations. Thus, if a client presents a number of dreams during the hour, the analyst looks for a common topic among them and if the client seems to jump from subject to subject, the analyst assumes that the same issue is being pursued (Spence 1982).

However important its role in open-ended treatments, thematic unity is especially prominent in brief psychotherapy. When time is short, therapist and client must focus on a unified theme under pain of dissipating the therapeutic effort. We have seen, for instance, how in Mann's (1973) time-limited therapy, the first therapeutic session ends in the formulation of the treatment's central issue. Mann's central issue offers a series of advantages for brief psychotherapy: it provides the therapy with a quick and engaging opening, is easy to remember and serves naturally as the organizer of therapeutic material. The reason for the formula's catchiness and organizing potential lies in its contrasting structure. Contrasts, as we know from cognitive psychology, are not only easily remembered, but also provide the scaffolding for our inner experience. We tend to pick up contrasts from any stimulus array and use them as the magnetic poles to which our mental fluff becomes attached.

Another thematic formula built on contrasting polarity was proposed by Omer (1993) to provide unity in eclectic therapy. One of the eclectic's hardest challenges is to steer the therapy between a symptom-oriented and a person-oriented direction. A therapy that wavers between the two risks fragmentation. On the other hand, if the therapist commits herself to one of these directions to the detriment of the other, the client's interest and motivation may dwindle. The *integrative focus* was designed to obviate this danger.

The integrative focus unifies the personal and the symptomatic themes so that both may be pursued together to their mutual advantage. The integrative formula is constituted by: (1.) a rationale for unifying the symptomatic and the personal foci; (2.) a statement establishing the two as symetrically related, so that progress in one is linked to progress in the other. For example: a student asked for treatment for a compulsion to align all objects in his flat, on pain of being punished with awful scholastic disasters (symptomatic focus). Additionally, he felt so dependent on his mother that he could hardly distinguish his own wishes from hers (personal focus). The treatment wavered, for a while, between these two themes, giving rise to a sense of diffusion. The following integrative focus pulled the two strands together:

(1.) In your touching behavior you describe a sense of being always intent on placating the gods. Feeling that you don't own your life, you must have recourse to these propitiatory rites to appease the rightful owners. The gods are very similar to your mother, whom you also try to appease by making the right choices. (2.) The compulsions and the dependency are the two sides of the same problem. In fighting the compulsions you will become better able to withstand your mother and to learn what you really want. On the other hand, in learning what you want and daring to face your mother, you will fortify yourself against the compulsions.

A Mother-in-Law Obsession

Susan's therapy was going well until she became obsessed with her mother-in-law. Since then, no progress could be made. Susan was 28 years old and lived with her husband in a religious (Jewish) neighborhood. When Susan was a child, her mother was taken to a mental hospital and this was the prelude to a series of hospitalizations that punctuated her childhood. The father never explained anything and the whole matter was kept under a cloud of secrecy. Susan was sent to a boarding-school where she always felt different and alone. In her teens she became interested in religion and attended courses in Judaica. In one of these she met David and they were married.

She sought therapy (with a religious therapist) because of her feelings of shame and inadequacy. Although very intelligent and eager to learn, she thought herself unfit for higher studies and consistently disparaged herself. She also felt deeply ashamed of her father for his boorish manners, and of her mother for her mental illness. Although she was highly conscientious in her care for her parents' welfare, she was too ashamed of them to allow them to visit her new home. She told no one, not even her husband, about her mother's illness.

Susan searched for perfection, morally, and spiritually. Her face beamed when she spoke of her religious studies. She yearned to make those values her own, to the point of viewing her personal shortcomings not as mere failings but as a betrayal of the true light. With the therapist's encouragement, Susan disclosed to David the secret of her mother's illness. To her surprise and joy, he not only was not angry but proved most supportive. She even went a step further and told the secret to her mother-in-law. Gradually, Susan was learning to appreciate her own assets, such as her perseverance and sensitivity. She became less demanding and more open with others and with herself until she found out to her dismay that her mother-in-law was a gossip.

Susan's life suddenly became centered on the mother-in-law. Once again her perfectionism and moralistic strain took the upper hand. Gossiping was, in her eyes, an unforgivable sin because it debased humanity and effaced its divine stamp. She was sure that her mother-in-law gossiped about her as she did about everyone else. She started to avoid her and would plan when to leave the house and when to come back so as not to meet her. She thought about nothing else. All other interests paled before the power of her aversion. It became impossible to talk of anything else in therapy.

The therapist searched unavailingly for a way to free Susan and the therapy from this obsession. She explored the possibility that Susan's major fear was that her mother-in-law would expose her secret. She interpreted Susan's aversion as linked to her anger towards her own mother. She tried to show Susan the positive sides of the mother-in-law (she was warm, generous, and joyful). Nothing helped; the mother-in-law had become an abomination in Susan's eyes. The therapist tried relaxation techniques, thought-stopping, alternative activities, but to no avail. At this point (after six months of progress and three months of impasse), the therapist brought the case to a group consultation with one of the authors.

The group explored the possibility that Susan's obsession stemmed from her difficult relationship with her own mother, who, besides being mentally ill, had always been very cold. Susan could not remember ever having received a kiss or a hug from her. Consequently she developed a highly charged attitude towards everything motherly. The viability of this hypothesis was supported when the therapist related that Susan had postponed all attempts to become pregnant until a month before. This was a highly unusual decision for a religious woman and it suggested that Susan was having considerable trouble with her own potential motherhood.

But, locked within her obsession, she seemed to be quite unresponsive to these interpretive lines. Therapy seemed to have become impaled on the horns of a dilemma. On one hand, Susan's acute distress precluded any gradual exploratory work that might link her obsession to her long-standing personal difficulties with motherhood and motherly figures; on the other hand, all attempts to deal symptomatically with the obsessions had failed. A way had to be found to pull these two strands, the symptomatic and the personal, together and an integrative focus was formulated. The symptomatic theme was defined as Susan's avoidance of her mother-in-law; the personal theme, as Susan's sense of an inner flaw. The following message embodies the group's attempt at thematic integration:

"In the wake of our last sessions I have reached some understanding about how your different problems may be related. Some of the things I have to say may be quite harsh and I think you may be shocked by them. Therefore, I want to give you also a summary in writing, so that you may review it at your own leisure.

"You grew up with a sense of a terrible flaw within you, which originated in your family and especially with your mother. You have tried to counter this sense of flaw by a constant search for higher values. This yearning, this spiritual and moral sense, you experience rightly as a very positive force within you. Because of these high standards, you abhor gossiping as an awful sin. However, this very abhorrence may be drawing you into a far graver sin: the sin of dehumanization. In banishing a gossip, you are also banishing a human being, your mother-in-law, declaring her unfit for human contact. You won't listen to her, visit her or eat with her. She talks too much and for this reason she stops being human and becomes an abomination in your eyes. You reject her and ostracize her. You turn her into a leper.

(Susan's own strict standards would probably make her responsive to such a harsh therapeutic split.)

"I believe that you are now faced with a double challenge. First, the need to revoke the banishment of your mother-in-law. You don't have to love her, but you must conquer your aversion. Second, the need to understand your sense of inner flaw, how it came about, how you may have gone too far in correcting it, and how you may come to terms with yourself. The two tasks are closely linked. As you learn to tolerate your mother-in-law, you will grow better able to understand and accept yourself; and as you learn to understand your sense of inner flaw and its tragic sources, you will become better able to tolerate your mother-in-law."

Susan was deeply affected. The obsession cleared up. She was much relieved by the therapist's saying that she was not obliged to love her mother-in-law. This made it easier for Susan to tolerate her. The therapy progressed also on the the personal front, which dealt with Susan's sense of inner flaw. After five months, however, the obsession returned.[1]

RECAPITULATION

Recapitulation is a Janus-headed combination of sameness and difference. The theme that reappears after a period of abeyance may be said to be both the same

1. The case is continued in the following section.

and not the same.[2] The intervening events create a new context that endows the theme's return with new significance. It is a truism that things are never what they were. The change however, is not necessarily for the worse. The Second Coming, for one, is supposed to be better than the First.

The past is continuously recreated. Schafer (1983) made this into a central tenet of his narrative approach. Each recollection involves a reconstruction and a reinterpretation. Our memories of childhood are no mere reproductions, but complex translations by the adult mind of what we believe to have happened. Thus, we often watch ourselves in the third person as actors in a scene we could never have witnessed. A memory of being cuddled by mother is different when recalled in a context of loneliness or in one of sexual failure. Growth and aging entail reevaluations: old trivia may become invaluable and past catastrophes ludicrous.

This transformation of the past in our attempts to preserve it is the central theme of Marcel Proust's (1981) masterpiece *Remembrance of Things Past.* The context of remembrance adds inevitably to what is remembered. In the act of remembering we sit astride time, living both in the present and in the past. For Proust, this is no loss. The meeting of the present with the past and the pattern that obtains from their intersection is a balm to our sense of finitude. Schafer

---

2. Our treatment of this issue is greatly indebted to Robert Rosenbaum's work. His unpublished manuscript *Music of the Mind* presents an analysis of the similarities between thematic return in psychotherapy and music. His seminal ideas in this respect were presented at the annual meeting of the American Psychological Association (Rosenbaum 1991).

speaks similarly about the spirality of memory in psychoanalysis; each recollection builds on previous ones. Schafer, like Proust, finds this inspiring; we are not fleeting nothings, peering longingly at dead events. On the contrary, we are time-giants atop our multi-layered past.

These musings have a practical import. When a client reappears with a problem we thought had been laid to rest, it seems as if the achievements of the therapy have been brought to naught. Perhaps, however, it is the relapse that is illusory. Indeed, the problem that returns or seems to do so is twice different. First, the client already knows the problem; second, he knows that he can do without it. Echoing Simone Signoret's famous saying that nostalgia is no longer what it was, we might say that neither is relapse. To reveal this similarity cum difference may be the challenge of psychotherapy in a recapitulation.

A Mother-in-Law Obsession (Conclusion)

> Susan arrived in despair; her obsession had returned. Once more she was filled with disgust at her mother-in-law. Once more, all her thoughts were taken with the woman's gossiping. The therapist, however, assumed that what seemed to be the same was not necessarily so, and she set out to search for what was new. Prompted by the therapist's questions, Susan told her that this time she had told David about her aversion for his mother's gossiping. Without a word to Susan, David told his mother that Susan was badly affected by her talkativeness. Deeply offended, she said she would not come to their house any longer. When David

reported this conversation to Susan, she was shocked. A family rift was afoot! And she was to blame! She went to her mother-in-law to beg her forgiveness, and it did not take long for the older woman to become reconciled. They embraced and Susan commented, "It was the first time in my life that I hugged anybody called mother." As Susan reached the end of her tale, it seemed hard to believe that she had started the session by complaining of a relapse.

The therapist told the consultation group that she felt the crisis could still take a bad turn. The group wondered what might have reawakened Susan's negative response. The therapist revealed that Susan was having trouble getting pregnant, and although she had tried for only six months, she was already quite sure that something was wrong with her. She doubted she would ever be able to become a mother. The therapist speculated that the return of the obsession might be linked to Susan's preoccupations with her own motherhood. The group proposed that a new integrative message be framed, playing on themes similar to the first. The following message was therefore formulated and delivered:

"You have made some big changes in your relationship with your mother-in-law: first, you apologized for the offense you had caused her; second, you chose to approach, rather than to avoid her. This is the best possible way to conquer the obsession. You have done something else of value—shown David that you are willing to go a long way to prevent a family rift.

"We have talked before about the connection between the obsession and your sense of inner flaw. This time, I believe, the return of the obsession was linked to your fear of being flawed in your potential motherhood.

For months you have been fearful about your ability to get pregnant. It is as if you were telling yourself that, with such a relationship with your two 'mothers,' you could not, yourself, become a mother. The pregnancy fears and your relation with your mothers are, of course, mutually linked. The more you succeed in opening up a personal space for your two mothers, the more you will be able to free that inner space from undue worries about pregnancy and motherhood. Conversely, as you develop a tolerant, patient, and accepting attitude towards pregnancy and motherhood, the easier it will be for you to be tolerant, patient, and accepting towards your two mothers."

Although the intervention was overtly directed at Susan's psychological attitude toward pregnancy, in the group there were hopes that the message might also affect her physiology. Susan, for her part, immediately detected this double-meaning in the message. Indeed, she became all the more willing to work on her attitude toward her mother-in-law (and her own mother) because she believed this might help her to get pregnant. The results justified the hopes; the obsession vanished. Nature helped too and Susan was soon pregnant.

(The therapeutic message underscored both the similarities and the differences between the present and previous manifestation of the problem. The chief similarity lay in the link between the obsession and Susan's sense of inner flaw. The chief difference lay in Susan's reaction, which was almost the opposite of what it had been [approach instead of avoidance.] Thus, the problem and the intervention were both the same and not the same. Susan could recognize her old self in her sense of flaw, her problematic relationship to mothers, and the obsession. On the other hand, there were new reactions, a new context, and new hopes. Therefore, it was a new Susan who figured in the new narrative.)

Variations

In thematic variations the focus of interest lies in the theme's diversification. There is often a growing tension created by the progressive distancing of each new variation from its thematic source. The story of Don Quixote, for instance, is a series of variations on the theme of the hero's estrangement from reality. There is a crescendo of absurdity in the Don's and Sancho's lordly reception at the duke's palace. When Don Quixote finally returns to his village, his homecoming is far more than a homecoming: he has become not only sane, but wise. Thus, the progressive distancing of the variations makes our return to the home theme into something that, though the same, is still vastly different.

But how? Have we not left psychotherapy far behind? What relationship can there be between the treatment of psychological problems and a literary succession of arabesques? Have we not been charmed by the narrative-literary analogy into realms that are far removed from the client's practical and painful concerns? Not so, we believe. Variations are called for wherever rigidity and uniformity reign unopposed. Their role is to loosen the oppressive hold of unchangeable, self-repeating patterns. They help us listen, think, feel, and act differently. Consider the following typical uses of variation forms in psychotherapy.

We have already alluded to Schafer's (1983) view that the spirality of narrative construction in psychoanalysis, in which similar events are retold from different viewpoints along the therapy, is an enriching therapeutic experience. With each new turn of the spiral, the client's view of self and life grows in flexibility. The whole therapy may then be considered as a set of variations on a few basic themes. Strategic and systemic therapists have made a similar point, underlining the analogic similarities behind the individual's symptomatic complaints, developmental problems, interpersonal relations, and family patterns (Haley 1977, Madanes 1981). The wiser treatment in this view is the one whose messages speak in as many of these tongues as possible, reverberating over multiple personal spheres at one time. One of Milton Erickson's major contributions to psychotherapy was precisely to transform the previously monochromatic lanuage of hypnosis into a polyphony of metaphoric allusions and varied elaborations on seemingly simple therapeutic themes (Erickson 1935, Erickson and Rossi 1979). Jungian therapists also make use of thematic variations not only by means of the client's own associations, but also by additional elaborations drawn from religion, art, and myth. Set in the context of such vast canvases, the client's once-petty problems are transformed into veritable spiritual odysseys.

Therapeutic variations may span the treatment as a whole or be developed focally, sometimes in a single session. Consider, for instance, the Milan School's procedure of circular interviewing (Selvini-Palazzoli et al. 1980). Whenever an important issue is described by a family member in a purportedly definitive way, the therapist encourages the other members to redescribe it from different angles and in different ways. For instance, the mother says that the problem is father's depression. The therapist may then ask the other members: "Who noticed the problem first?" "For whom is it less of a problem?" "For whom is it not a problem at all?" "What happens to mother and eldest daughter when father stays in bed?" "What happens to them when father goes back to work?" "How do the other children react to the changes in mother?" By the end of the session, the static picture of father's depression has been turned into a shifting kaleidoscope.

Variation forms also supply an effective structure for a session of guided imagery. For instance, after the client has visualized a problematic situation, he may be encouraged to do so repeatedly, within varying contexts and with different outcomes (Erickson 1970). For example, a client came to one of us complaining that ever since he had been injured in a terrorist attack he lived in constant fear of bombs. He could not walk around for fear of bombs, worried constantly for the safety of his wife and daughters and woke up nightly drenched in urine. Two previous therapists had given up on him because all he talked about in therapy was his fear of bombs and even this in an extremely stereotyped manner. In the course of a few sessions, I asked him to have a series of waking dreams about bombs, making changes each time in the scenery, the cast, or the outcome. The initial dreams were very much alike and replicated the original trauma in great detail. Soon, however, he started to provide more daring variations. He dreamt, for instance, that he was driving a bus in which a bomb was found and although he succeeded in getting all the passengers out, he remained trapped inside the bus, which careened on its own down a serpentine road. Or, that his wife had been to the market and, hidden among the cauliflowers in her basket, he found a hand grenade. Thereupon, he started to yell and beat her furiously. Or, that he was flying in the clouds, happy and secure, watching the dangerous streets below. Gradually, he became able not only to talk about the dreams freely, but also to imagine situations that were more and more different from the original one. This newly gained flexibility in imagery was soon followed by other improvements. The nocturnal enuresis stopped and he started to move about more freely.[3]

Besides endowing the client's patterns with flexibility, variation forms also enhance the impact of the therapist's communications. By relaying our messages through a variety of channels, we increase the chances that they will capture attention, register effectively in the client's mind and remain available in times of need (Omer 1990, 1992, 1994, Omer et al. 1993). Indeed, variation is a far better procedure for achieving impact than is simple repetition, for whereas repetition leads rapidly to habituation, variation does not (Omer 1987). Additionally, variation forms address different channels of receptivity; a client who is impervious to a given form of one message may be receptive to another. Channel multiplicity is an obvious advantage in family therapy, where one form of the message may be appropriate to the mother, still another to the father, and another to the children. In one example by Minuchin and Fishman (1981), the parents of four teenagers were instructed to talk to each other directly about their disagreements, instead of addressing the therapist. The

3. Fate, however, still held a more ghastly variation; ten years after the treatment, his eldest daughter was killed in a terrorist attack.

proposal was met with generalized laughter by the four children. Apparently, direct conversation between the parents was highly uncommon in this family. The therapist insisted, blocked the parents' addresses to himself, gestured to create an imaginary partition between the parents and the children, turned the parents' seats so they faced each other, looked out the window to prevent eye contact, moved a child's seat away so that it faced one of another sibling, and instructed the parents to invite the children to comment only when both parents agreed to allow this. Each of these ways of conveying the message affected the family in a different way and the whole lot had a cumulative effect. What had seemed risible, at start, became a reality.

We shall not present an extended case illustrating the use of variations as a form of thematic elaboration, because we have done so already. The case of Ofra (Chapter 2) is a set of variations on the dual theme of combat and acceptance. The need to work on this theme arose quite early in the treatment, when the therapist was faced with the potential damage caused by Ofra's uncritical embracing of the Simmontons' (1981) optimistic message, according to which, getting well again was totally a function of her own psychological attitude. Although this doctrine usually strengthened her, whenever there was a medical setback Ofra would blame herself for it most harshly. To help Ofra through the critical challenges that the malady would inevitably pose to her, therapy had to counterbalance the one-sided message of the Simmontons (1981) with another one, aiming at acceptance of setbacks and external help. The double theme of combat and acceptance was geared toward this end. A series of variations on this theme were offered to help Ofra face a variety of crises: (1.) the hypnotic dissociation into a part that knew what was going on, and a part that felt differently; (2.) the story of Fabius' and Scipio's fight against Hannibal, in which a strategy of retreat was combined with a plan of attack; (3.) the use of Demolition Man as a metaphor for the need to accept external help, with all its attendant risk of hurt and damage when faced with one's limitations; (4.) the paradoxical time frame of General Raful's battles in the War of Liberation and the Yom Kippur War, where five minutes turned into twenty-five years, but where twenty-five years were also actually five minutes. In each of these images, there is a dialectical interplay between two apparently contradictory ideas: knowing one way and feeling another, attacking and retreating, being hurt and being helped, experiencing the brevity and the length of time. Each image spoke to Ofra's need to accept and to go on fighting; to hope and to resign herself. In the very final metaphor, Ofra was crowned with the laurels of the victorious Citadel, at the very moment of her body's actual defeat.

CONTRAPOSITION

We once heard a client say, "Therapy, therapy, quite contrerapy!" She was voicing a common feeling. Therapists are often expected to go for the contrary (clients who thought they loved their parents often find out that they really hate them and vice-versa) and many of our dearest theoretical notions are polarized (conscious-unconscious, symbiosis–individuation, love–hate, yes–but). Contraposition is so ubiquitous in psychotherapy that we are obliged to delimit our scope in describing its uses. We chose to focus on one broad category of polarized interventions, which Omer (1991) has termed dialectical. A dialectical intervention embodies two opposed themes or moves (thesis and antithesis) that, as the focus shifts from the one to the other, drama and change are mobilized. Sometimes the thematic opposition is left as such, the very swing serving as a lever for change; sometimes the opposition gives rise to a synthesis. Consider the following examples.

In some forms of strategic therapy, the client (or family) is faced with two therapists, the one pessimistic and obnoxious, the other optimistic and supportive (Hoffman, Gafni and Laub 1994). The bad therapist criticizes the client and demands a strict treatment regimen. The good therapist, often silent at the beginning, slowly emerges as the client's paladine, supporting her rights for independence, participation, and trust. The therapeutic pendulum swings, of course, towards the "good" therapist.

In the two-chair technique of Gestalt therapy, a client who displays two opposite tendencies is asked to role-play one of them first, and then the other. The client is enjoined not to choose between the two but to own up to both (a synthesis suggestion). Similarly, in the odd-and-even-days ritual developed by the Milan School (Tomm 1984), when a couple disagrees over a major issue, they are told that one of them is to have his way on odd days of the week and the other on even days. On Sundays, the couple is to act spontaneously (again, a synthesis suggestion).

Sometimes, thesis and antithesis are played out in two separate therapeutic stages. Such a two-stage format was used by one of us for treating families with rebellious teenagers in which neither the parents nor the youngster were willing to compromise. The parents (usually the interested party) would be asked whether they were ready for an all-out fight for their principles. If they declared themselves willing (they invariably did), they would have to commit themselves bindingly to a strenuous six-week treatment effort. The program would include taking the child to school and back (when truancy was a problem), sitting with him for homework, staying with him throughout the weekend, and monitoring his daily schedule. Sometimes, the youngster would not be left alone for a single moment during the entire six weeks. Conflicts were rife and both parties would become invariably drained by the end of this period. Softened by exhaustion, both sides would usually be ready for a second therapeutic stage characterized by negotiation and compromise.

Seesaw

Ilana and Uri, both in their thirties, were heading towards divorce. Uri was a psychologist with a home practice, who also taught at the university. He was also in charge of most of the housekeeping. Ilana directed a travel agency and worked long hours every day. She could not bear what she viewed as Uri's manipulative psychologizing. Uri, on his side, felt terrorized by Ilana's smoldering anger and recurrent hysterical outbursts. At times she would scream so loudly that the neighbors would knock on the walls to make her stop.

Both were in therapy and their individual therapists had agreed to their coming for a number of marital sessions with one of the authors.

Uri talked in a highly convoluted manner. Only by strenuous effort could I understand his description of Ilana. He saw her as a land mine about to explode. He feared that sooner or later she would physically harm someone in the family. Ilana saw everything in a completely different light. She had gone to therapy, hoping, among other things, to change her difficult relationship with Uri and learn how to get closer to their children. In her view, Uri was actuated by the need to control her and keep the children on his side. He would never acknowledge this, she complained, and all the blame was invariably shifted to her. "Whenever I try to say something to him, he psychologizes and ends up throwing the problem back at me. I don't need him as a therapist; I have my own! How dare he interpret my behavior if he doesn't even listen to me?" Besides, Uri controlled the children, leaving her no place and no influence. Every initiative of hers became trammeled up in his net.

Uri, on his side, said he wanted Ilana to take the initiative and make her presence positively felt at home. But she always came to him with strict demands that she wanted put into practice, forthwith. He needed time to consider, but she invariably pushed for an immediate decision. Ilana countered that she was fed up with his evasiveness. The two views were mutually exclusive. What seemed as a step forward to one of them was a backward step to the other. Therapy was in constant danger of veering towards one view at the expense of the other. Such development would probably bring Uri and Ilana closer to divorce. Unless the two versions were given similar weight, the therapy would disintegrate.

The following messsage, delivered to the couple at the start of the second session, reflects this need for balance:

"I understand, Uri, that in your dealings with Ilana, anxiety is the ruling factor. You are frightened by her outbursts and perhaps even more by her pent-up anger. You have learned to deal with your anxiety by evasiveness, hoping to preclude or at least postpone the conflagration. That is why your style of speaking is so evasive; you are using language as a delay mechanism. Experience has taught you that any attempt to be more direct would be met only with more rage. I fear, however, that your very attempt at self-protection is experienced by Ilana as manipulative. When I listen to the way you talk, I can understand her reaction. Sometimes it is very hard to know what you want and there is a feeling that you are weaving a net of words to trap her. Ilana's outbursts may perhaps be precipitated by that feeling.

"As for you, Ilana, your dominant feeling as I understand it is that Uri makes you helpless. You want your voice to be heard in the family, but you feel it is consistently neutralized. Deprived of your voice, you shout. Unable to be firm, you become aggressive. To my mind your anger is the outward form of your helplessness. Uri is so blinded by your anger that he fails to see the underlying despair. Moreover, when I hear you talking, I understand his fear, for in spite of your efforts at self-control, you vibrate with rage. No wonder he is anxious; no wonder you feel trapped.

"I think you are both right in what you feel, but mistaken in what you see. Ilana, if you could perceive the anxiety under Uri's evasiveness, you would be able to reduce it. Uri, if you could see the helplessness behind Ilana's anger, you would be able to remedy it."

The therapeutic split did not at first seem to work as expected. Each side agreed eagerly to the good things I had said about one and the bad things I had said about the other. Each spouse felt I had understood his or her own suffering, but had failed to see into the dark recesses of the other. I told them that time would show if either of them was right. In the meantime, we had a double task at hand: Uri must learn to deal with his fear of Ilana's aggressiveness, and Ilana must make her voice heard, despite Uri's attempts to muffle it up with wooly verbiage. I offered to begin with Uri; Ilana would help by supplying the anger.[4] I taught Uri to relax and asked Ilana to say everything she had ever wanted to say to him, without mincing her words. Uri was to keep his eyes and mouth shut; his job was to focus on his anxiety and witness how it would grow, but then, inevitably, diminish. Ilana spoke for a long time. She chose the worst of words and the worst of tones, growing hoarse with anger. "You never listen to me! I count for nothing in your eyes! You have put a wall between us! You have incited the children against me! You have painted me as a monster in their eyes and posed before them as a martyr and a saint! You cannot begin to imagine what a hypocrite you are!" Uri would move restlessly in his seat, open his eyes, and try to answer back. I would interrupt him, saying that our goal was not to decide who was right, but how he could stop being ruled by anxiety. We would interrupt the procedure until Uri relaxed, and Ilana could begin anew. This procedure lasted three sessions. Uri became

4. This technique of having one member of the couple train the other in withstanding his own problematic reactions was described in detail by Lange (1989).

less and less emotional about Ilana's attacks and Ilana more and more tired of screaming the same accusations.

We then focused on Ilana's lack of a firm voice at home. Between sessions she was to think about what she wanted to say on various family issues. During the sessions she was to voice her thoughts clearly and firmly. Uri was to try to entangle her by psychological haziness and filibuster. He would attribute Ilana's position to her personal problems, dig up events from the distant past, change the subject and confuse the issue. Ilana learned to stick to her point, without screaming.

Gradually, they came to perceive the connection between the two patterns. Uri's anxiety and Ilana's helplessness began to appear as the two sides of the same problem. The more Uri was anxious, the more evasive he became, making Ilana grow angrier. Conversely, Ilana's helplessness deepened her sense of impotent rage, causing Uri to become more anxious. The treatment of Uri's anxiety helped Ilana gain control over her outbursts, and training of Ilana to firmness and self-control offered Uri a better grasp of his convoluted speech. Uri's and Ilana's seemingly unbridgeable realities were thus brought under a common conceptual and therapeutic roof. This new unity found its first concrete manifestation when Uri and Ilana succeeded in planning together for a sabbatical abroad. They were away for a year, which they described as a difficult, but positive, family experience.

(The disjointed perspectives which had, in the past, led to independent therapies and to a centrifugal trend in the marriage were brought together, first in a symmetric formulation of the problem and, then, in an integrative synthesis. Therapy wound up with one central, circular theme. Thematic contraposition may thus become an instrument for achieving thematic unity.)

Unfortunately, things eventually got out of hand and Uri filed for divorce. At present Uri and Ilana are trying to reach an agreement with the help of a divorce mediator. Our elegant symmetrical achievement turned out to be short-lived.

5

MEANINGS

A meaningful therapeutic narrative must fulfill three conditions, allowing the client to say: (1.) This is my story; (2.) I am the hero of this story; and (3.) This story has a future. The client must recognize herself fully in the narrative; otherwise she will experience a sense of self-estrangement. She must feel she is the heroine or major progatonist; otherwise she will suffer from a sense of passiveness and marginality. She must feel that the narrative offers her options; otherwise she will be condemned to despair. Often clients come to us with a life-story that fails them on all three counts. Thus, they may feel that their narrative was handed to them by their betters or by providence, that it turns their lives into an appendage to the lives of others or into the debris of an indifferent conflagration, and that it leaves them without a purpose or an option. Such narratives are experienced as empty of meaning.

Traditionally, psychotherapy has always dealt with meanings but in a different sense. The typical therapeutic question used to be: What is the meaning of this dream, symptom, or slip of the tongue? Though often hidden, the meaning was supposed to be objectively there. This belief has been termed the assumption of *the one true meaning* (Omer and Strenger 1992). It was abetted by the belief that there was only one right perspective for disclosing true meanings. This was the assumption of *God's point of view* (Omer and Strenger 1992). Both beliefs are now much less accepted than in the past. Their rejection underlies the anti-positivist revolution that has spawned the narrative approach. Today, we hardly talk to our clients about *the* true meaning of their behavior. We talk instead of meanings that emerge in conversation and are made acceptable by consensus (explicit or tacit). It is, thus, a consensus endorsed by most therapists and clients that meanings that are conducive to a sense of self-recognition, agency, and purpose are therapeutic. Conversely, meanings that are conducive to a sense of self-estrangement, passivity, and despair are anti-therapeutic. In this chapter we explore these criteria of therapeutic meaningfulness.[1] We attempt to depict

1. Some philosophers (e.g., Baier 1981) distinguish between meaning and significance. Thus, the sentence, "The cat is on the mat," has meaning but little significance. In the transition from the objective meanings of positivist psychotherapy into the construed meanings of the narrative approach, we might say that there is a shift in emphasis from meaning to significance. This chapter deals with significance.

some of the many forms of meaninglessness with which our clients confront us. On our way, we shall stumble on a paradox; the client may become so saddled with his own or his therapist's demands for meaningfulness, that a pinch of meaninglessness may prove salutary.

THIS IS MY STORY

When a person says, "This is my story," she is expressing a sense of self-recognition. The face in the story looks like her own; events carry her stamp; the story is transparent to the self, unlike the stories of others. If asked, "What is so special about your story?" she might answer, "It is mine!"

This experience can be clarified by attending to its reverse, the feeling that somehow, "This is not my story." The person may feel that she is playing a role attached to her from the outside; that her life is a series of acts performed in obeisance to an external injunction; that the shoes she wears are not really hers; that her motions have an automatic feel; that her beliefs seem dictated and her feelings implanted. Life becomes meaningless because it is not experienced as her own.

Many of us have, at times, played with the idea that our lives may be a show put on by others. They are in the know, and maybe someday they will lift the curtain. Such a fantasy has been engagingly depicted in John Fowles's novel *The Magus* (1966). Throughout the story, the narrator, who is also the main protagonist, feels that the events around him have been staged by someone who is most intimately acquainted with the protagonist's life. Everything that happens refers to his own feelings, thoughts, memories, and plans. Most strangely, except for him, everyone seems to be in the know. Tolstoy, in *My Confession* (1905), has described a similar experience. Like the hero of *The Magus*, Tolstoy had the feeling that others (the peasants) knew well what it was all about. He, alone, could not find his way into the secret.

A similar feeling of dispossession may arise when our experience is disconfirmed by others or when we are coached on how to think or feel. Thus, when we are told that things are not as we see them, that we are perverted, psychotic, possessed, or more insiduously that we are defensive or insensitive, we may come to disbelieve our very experience.

Gripped by inner doubts, a client may approach his therapist with a pressing need for confirmation: "Say that I am right, that things are really like that, that I am not dreaming!" A delicate moment, for the therapist may not see eye to eye with him. One solution that has occasionally been advocated in the history of psychotherapy is for the therapist to develop a fully acceptant attitude, a readiness to follow the client wherever he may lead, like an anthropologist finding her way in a new culture. Sometimes, however, this will simply not do. Not only because the therapist is unable to suppress her own position, but also because the client refuses to be satisfied with bland, impersonal confirmation, demanding, instead, a full-blooded interlocutor. The sympathetic anthropologist may thus be cornered by point-blank questions like: "Do you feel like me? Would you do likewise?" or the embarrassing: "Will you tell my wife and my lawyer that you think so, too?"

Indeed, many of those inestimable moments in which we feel a sense of self-confirmation, when the world feels newly painted with our look, may be made possible only through our encounter with such a full-blooded other, and sometimes through his lead. Take for instance, those moments of discovery of the self-revealing power of poetry, when we are almost brought to exclaim: "How does the poet know these things about me?" Or, when we are shaken out of a lethargic, unfeeling state by the push of a friend that makes us say: "I had forgotten how it feels to be myself!"

We believe that expecting the client to become the sole author of his life is both unrealistic and burdensome. The client knows full well that not every description of himself conveyed by another, even if unpleasant, should or could be shaken off. At times, it is precisely the stubborn refusal of another to accept our acts or even our thoughts and feelings, that rekindles hope and points the way to a saving change. Not everything good comes from the self-authoring I.

MEDITATION

One of the authors occasionally received referrals of youngsters who found themselves confused on their return from the Far East. One of these was a young man who behaved quite oddly. He stared constantly ahead, moved with agonizing slowness, never spoke unless spoken to and even then replied cryptically, puzzling his parents and friends. When people asked him about his plans for the future, he would answer that he did not exist, or that planning was a delusion. He was taken to two psychiatrists; one diagnosed him as suffering from schizophrenia, the other, from psychotic depression. He was also taken to a psychotherapist, but he would not speak. After one session with each of these three practitioners he refused to see them again. He agreed to come to me because he knew I had been to India and was familiar with Buddhism. As he sat down across from me, staring intently ahead, I thought he might be trying to meditate. I asked him if he was meditating. He said he was. I asked him whether he was finding it difficult to keep meditating in his new surroundings. He said he was. This initial interchange, however meager, established the possibility of a dialogue, for he could recognize himself in the terms I was using. Even this youngster, apparently so intent on keeping himself isolated from everyone, yearned for confirmation.

Gradually, he unfroze a bit. He would, for instance, curtly correct my attempts to guess what was going on inside him. In our second session, he volunteered that he wanted to go on meditating but feared he would go crazy. Although he remained laconic, my guesses became more guided. We started a dialogue about flexible and rigid practices of meditation. If I went too far with my guessing, his reactions would help me to retrace my steps. For instance, in trying to soften his rigid self-demands, I gave him the example of a master who would hit him with a bamboo stick whenever his mind went astray. I asked him if such a master would help him. He said he would become even more distracted. I then asked him about another master who would smile to encourage him whenever he opened his eyes in moments of trouble. He answered tentatively, "Well, I feel he should be firm enough to keep me just. . . ." He would say no more, but from his broken sentence I gathered that he was not recognizing himself in the image I had offered. I made a short methodic break to think things over. He seemed to need an image that exuded firmness as well as approval. When I came back a few minutes later, I told him that I had reflected on what he had said. He was right that firmness and even harshness might be very important in creating the right conditions for meditation such as keeping a schedule, maintaining a proper diet, living simply. However, the wild horse cannot be tamed by force, nor can the mind; you cannot educate it by blows. The right target for strict demands were the surrounding conditions and not the meditation itself. Here, flexibility was necessary. He agreed and from then on I was able to stay closer to him. He gradually shook off most of his strange behavior. He learned to accept that, far from providing him with the right conditions to meditate, his queer acts were only frightening his parents and even himself. He started to walk and talk normally. He continued to meditate for a few hours every day, but he also resumed his studies at the university. He developed a plan on how to maintain his Buddhism. Once a year he would go on a retreat. The rest of the year he would keep up his Buddhist practices in the hours he had stipulated, but would live regularly, otherwise. This life-narrative was quite different from the one he had been trying to develop when he arrived. I had been an active partner in its construction, but it was no less his for that reason; he had guided me and I had guided him.

It is sometimes implied in the literature that all would be well if the client established his authorship or reowned his narrative. Bad things, it would seem, can only happen if the narrative is slipped upon one from the outside. This view tends to attribute all problems to an external conspiracy. We disagree. We find that people can be highly imaginative in fixing themselves nasty narratives. Throughout this book, we have argued that through an empathic effort we can recognize the inner logic of even the most abstruse-seeming piece of behavior. However, this recognition does not entail our closing our eyes to its negative effects. Damage is damage, even when autonomously storied. Therapy is not only about establishing narrative ownership but also about developing more helpful stories.

I AM THE HERO OF THIS STORY

Let us begin with the reverse experience: how does one feel as the non-hero of one's story? How can a person say that her life narrative is not mainly about her? In many ways: the person may experience herself as a cog in a machine, as a creature of habit, as an appendage to someone else, as too weak for effort, as determined by the past, as too stupid to know what is good for her, as too abject for improvement, as at the mercy of blind drives, as governed by the body, as driven by norms, or as a fleck of dust amidst the galaxies. Endless novels and philosophical works have been dedicated to these experiences.

By its emphasis on pathology and on the rule of the past, psychotherapy has often abetted these experiences; by its emphasis on self-knowledge and eventual self-determination, it has called them into question. Modern critics of classical psychotherapy have tended to stress its pessimistic and deterministic side. A closer look, however, reveals that each of the classical approaches has put forward its own heroic image of the person. Classical psychoanalysis, side by side with its dark view of humankind as dominated by blind, unconscious drives, has upheld an ideal of uncompromising honesty and growing awareness. These expectations were directed both at the client and the therapist. Far from unheroic, we find them promethean in scope. Behavior therapy, although much blamed for its deterministic reductionism, has preached an active militantism, centered on the present. These demands extended also to the therapist, bringing him out of the clinic and into the world as an active partner in the client's struggle. The previous generation of family therapists has been criticized for its emphasis on homeostatic forces, the overruling importance of structure, and the inductive power of enmeshment. Nonetheless, it presented an inspiring ideal of individuation, protected each member from being completely absorbed into the family, and countered tendencies at pathological labeling and scapegoating. Therefore, in this respect the modern narrative and constructive approaches, far from revolutionary, are joining a respectable tradition.

We would not take the trouble of stressing this continuity were it not that some narrativists, inflamed by a belief that they are the first to raise the banner of self-definition, have been led to a totalist ethos of embattled autonomy. But what if the client feels uninclined to fight? What if she does not identify with the ideal of self-liberation? What if she has a penchant for acceptance and compromise? What if fate plays a trump card? There is little place in the modern terminology of self-reclaiming and self-authoring for respite and resignation. We should remember that we live in the age of the anti-hero. Why not broaden our heroic scope so as to include in our pantheons also heroes and heroines who are resigned, self-effacing, pathetic, tragic, quixotic, or just simply tired? Have we learned nothing from Charlie Chaplin's tramp or Graham Greene's whiskey priest? These marvelous models have taught us how humanity and defeat may be the closest of bedfellows. Let us return for a moment to the experiences of meaninglessness that opened this section. Are they worthless? Should we merely help our clients to overcome them, lay them aside, attribute them to a conspiracy that recruited them into viewing themselves in a negative light, and learn instead how to focus on solutions? Not so, we believe. We need these experiences to tame our hubris. Take, for instance, the experience that Yalom (1980) has termed *the galactic perspective* (the feeling that results from considering our insignificant place in the cosmos). Douglas Adams, in his hilarious *The Restaurant at the End of the Universe,* turned the galactic perspective into the ultimate torture by embodying it in a machine that presented, totally and immediately to the victim's awareness, his size vis-à-vis the whole universe. The ordeal invariably crushed the victim into psychological pulp. Fortunately in real life we keep forgetting the galactic perspective. We dip into it at times but are rescued by daily demands. But, do we come back the same? Not if we are wise. In Nagel's (1971) beautiful phrase, we return to our lives, as we must, but our seriousness is laced with irony.

THIS STORY HAS A FUTURE

Among the faces of meaninglessness, perhaps the most familiar to the modern mind is the one symbolized by

Albert Camus's Sisyphus (1955), who is forever doomed to roll a stone to the top of a hill and to have his efforts brought to naught by the stone's rolling down when the summit is reached. Thus, for Camus the human condition is unredeemable toil, devoid of purpose, value, or redemption. There are many paths leading people to the sisyphean outook: some are struck by an overwhelming sense of pointlessness; some feel inexorably bound by senseless chains; some feel that life is all wishing, with no satisfaction. In all of these conditions the world is experienced as alien, hostile, and absurd.

The ideal solution for this malady seems to be the discovery of an absolute purpose or total meaning, such as is sometimes found in faith, dedication to a cause, love, or creativity. Interestingly, seekers for total meaning have a decided preference for the singular; they speak of *the* meaning, rather than of meanings. Frankl's (1963) famous book is entitled *Man in Search of Meaning*, not *meanings*. It seems as if a purpose would not be meaningful enough unless it were only one. A plurality of goals would spoil all by smuggling in the worm of relativity. Besides, plurality would dissipate the exhilaration of having a single meaning take hold of one's life. Psychotherapy often echoes this totality: *Meaning*, *Purpose*, and *Engagement* are singularized, capitalized, and italicized. The demand may be inspiring, but it may also become paralyzing. Couldn't we, sometimes, make do without this totality?

Reconsider Sisyphus. One humane interpreter (Taylor 1970) has proposed a slight change in his punishment. Suppose that as a merciful afterthought the gods had decided to implant in him an irrational impulse to roll stones. Suppose that he is so obsessed with that wish that the moment he gets one stone to the top of the hill, he wants to roll another up. Sisyphus's fate no longer appears to him as a condemnation. On the contrary: he is now guaranteed endless fulfilment of his chief desire. Remember that Sisyphus's labor is still not imbued with a final purpose, for nothing comes out of his stonerolling. No temple emerges, no final meaning crowns his labor. The stones keep rolling back. And yet, Sisyphus is reconciled. We believe that this is precisely what happens when the question of meaninglessness seems to be resolved: the sufferer develops an interest in rolling stones.

Such a solution might sound cynical. We have solved Sisyphus's problem by having him resign himself to the tyranny of the gods! What a betrayal of the lucid rebel within us! Camus's hero would rather be destroyed while shaking his fist in the face of the nonexistent gods! A Sisyphus who is so easily cheated out of his fight would merit his dismal fate. To become engrossed in the push and the shove! To forget himself in meaningless action! But is it so? Is the obsession with rolling stones less worthy than a putative temple of meaning at its end? What would happen to a busy-minded Sisyphus were the temple to be finished? He would die of boredom! Or worse, be forced to continue living in the contemplation of the lofty goal that deprived him of his beloved occupation! Indeed, a Sisyphus obsessed with rolling stones is no mean figure. On the contrary, there is nobility in becoming so engrossed with one's acts as to forget about their final purpose. No one has expressed this better than the Greek poet Cavafy:

> As you set out for Ithaka
> hope your road is a long one,
> full of adventure, full of discovery . . .
>
> Keep Ithaka always in your mind.
> Arriving there is what you're destined for.
> But don't hurry the journey at all.
> Better if it lasts for years,
> so you're old by the time you reach the island,
> wealthy with all you've gained on the way,
> not expecting Ithaka to make you rich.
> Ithaka gave you the marvelous journey.
> Without her you wouldn't have set out.
> She has nothing left to give you now.
> And if you find her poor, Ithaka won't have
> fooled you.
> Wise as you will have become, so full of
> experience,
> you'll have understood by then what these
> Ithakas[2] mean.
>
> (1975, p. 35)

We hope that in the treatments and consultations brought together in this book we have given our client-heroes the possibility of also displaying a strain of the anti-hero. We hope we may have helped them find some relief from an excessive thirst for the

2. There is a plural to our taste!

absolute. We hope we may have lightened somewhat their unbearable heaviness of meaning and that they have not found the lightness uninspiring.

TRAUMA, MEANING, AND CONTINUITY

Trauma is a great destroyer of meaning. Victims of trauma have been described in the literature as undergoing a temporary disruption in the ability to make sense of events or a breakdown of their meaning-making assumptions (Horowitz 1986, Janoff-Bulman 1985). Along these lines, Wigren (1994) has proposed that the traumatic effect of an experience is directly linked to the victim's inability to organize it by chains of meaning, thus endowing it with narrative form. In this view, traumatic memories are not a story at all, but a collection of disconnected fragments, of sensorial-physiological snapshots, which are mentally disruptive precisely because they are formless. This view of post-traumatic conditions is different from the classical one that has dominated professional literature since the publication of Breuer and Freud's (1895–1955) *Studies in Hysteria*. Whereas in the classical version, the traumatic narrative is repressed *en bloc*, and treatment consists of its abreactive recovery, in Wigren's interpretation, there is no narrative to begin with. Trauma consists precisely in the breakdown of the story-making ability that makes experience assimilable. Wigren proposed that the role of treatment is to help the client construct for the first time the story of the trauma.

Recently we (Omer and Alon 1994) have laid similar emphasis on the function of continuity in the treatment of trauma. We have stressed, however, that traumatic experiences are not only those that are, in themselves, unstoried and fragmented, but also those that shatter the frame of a person's overall life-narrative. Consider the following: (1.) a religious Jew who, after the Holocaust loses all belief in providence; (2.) a prisoner of war who reveals military secrets. In both cases, major narrative continuities have been disrupted, even though the traumatic events in themselves may be well-organized in orderly narratives. The task of reestablishing continuity between the broken parts of these individuals' life-narratives may then be far more crucial than that of reordering the traumatic experience in itself. Indeed, many of the clients we have treated suffered rather from an inability to fit their traumatic stories into the flow of their narratives of self and world than from the chaotic fragmentation of the traumatic experience as such. All in all, we would say that in the treatment of traumatic conditions it is vital to help the client establish continuity wherever the breach is most acutely experienced. In some cases this will include the traumatic events in themselves; in others, not at all. Indeed, a therapist's insistence that the client should invariably be helped to reprocess the trauma may actually increase her sense of helplessness and victimization (Durrant and Kowalski 1990). In effect, continuity is the basis of meaningfulness. It is impossible to say of a shattered narrative: This is my story, I am the hero of this story, and this story has a future. We believe that the acutest sense of traumatic disruption will be felt precisely at those points in the narrative where these three conditions of meaningfulness are invalidated.

The present view helps us make sense of some perplexing findings about people with post-traumatic conditions. In a series of studies conducted in The Sleep Laboratories of the Technion in Haifa about the dream-patterns of Holocaust survivors and war victims, a clear trend revealed that subjects who were asymptomatic were less able than symptomatic individuals to report dreams when awakened during their REM periods, even when those dreams included traumatic elements. The same was true about their war memories: the symptomatic subjects were better able to relate in a full, orderly manner than were the asymptomatic ones. Apparently it is not simply the lack of narrative order in the traumatic events themselves that makes for a post-traumatic stress syndrome. Following our narrative interpretation, we would propose that war trauma had not disrupted the sense of self, agency, and purpose of the asymptomatic subjects. Their life narratives were reconnected after the war, allowing for a sense of personal continuity. The symptomatic subjects, on the other hand, were those whose trauma had split the overall narrative line. Even if their war experiences could be remembered and related in orderly fashion, their life-narratives had been broken, not allowing for a sense of recognition, centrality, and purpose. In what follows we shall present two cases of war trauma. In both, the trauma narrative itself and its connecting links to the overall life-narrative played different roles. Both will serve as illustrations of the three conditions for a meaningful therapeutic narrative.

The Trial

David fell captive to the Egyptians in the Yom Kippur War. He was 19. When his tank commander was wounded, he tried to radio for help but bungled the connection. The commander died in his arms. He planned to die fighting rather than be taken captive, but his determination failed him. He was tortured, raped, kept in solitary confinement and twice led to fake executions. He returned to Israel in an awful state. He felt he had disgraced the Israeli Army and his family name. He blamed himself for the death of his commander and for his own capture. He suffered from nightmares, intrusive memories, excruciating headaches, and delusions that the Mossad and the Egyptians were after him. He became addicted to tranquilizers. His ability to concentrate deteriorated and he found himself leaving one place of work after another. He talked to no one except his father with whom he lived and with whom he fought all the time. He looked haggard and dishevelled. The Ministry of Defense recognized him as psychiatrically disabled and awarded him a pension.

David was referred to one of the authors for treatment nine years after the war. I tried to help him control his intrusive memories by means of hypnosis. The major treatment effort, however, was directed at his daily life. I supported him in his desire to leave his father's home and rent a small apartment. We developed a program to bring him back to work (with limited success) and to decrease his isolation. In a few months he started to socialize, met a divorced woman with two children and married her. Since he was jobless most of the time, he took care of the house and the children. He dressed them, fed them, read them stories, doted on them, and pampered them. In his eagerness to buy them toys and clothes, he once took advantage of a checkbook he had found in the street.

David's relationship with his wife was very strained.

They had frequent fights and she would often become extremely abusive. Still, family life imparted some sense and steadiness to his existence. He took odd jobs here and there and always talked about the children. The war seemed very distant, and our meetings became less frequent. About two years after his marriage, however, David was visited by a horrible tragedy. His younger stepdaughter climbed over the windowsill and fell to her death from the third floor. David was racked with pain and guilt. Rationally, he knew he was not to blame, especially since he had ordered a safety grid installed, but his wife had cancelled the order for financial reasons. Still, he blamed himself. He became depressed, the war memories returned in all their awful intensity, and to cap it all his wife divorced him. We were back to square one. David felt he had been condemned to lifelong suffering because of his assumed guilt.

Soon after these tragic events, I left the country for a year and David joined a group of other disabled war veterans in a program organized by the Ministry of Defense. While abroad I began thinking that we had never really addressed David's self-accusations on the matter of his captivity and of his commander's death. Because of the chaos that ruled throughout the Yom Kippur War and after it, there had never been an orderly inquiry into the events that had led to his captivity. On his return to Israel he had been treated from the start as a psychiatric casualty and, actually, was never reintegrated into the army he felt he had disgraced. I decided that on my return, I would try to correct this mistake. I felt especially close to him, since I was also attempting to come to terms with events that had happened to me when I was on active combat duty.

(What the therapist wanted to achieve was not an abreaction of the war experiences but a real and, if possible, official inquiry and

rehabilitation that might help retie the strands of his broken life narrative. In fact, David could relate his war experiences perfectly well. Furthermore, the group treatment he had undergone had been based on abreaction and elaboration of the trauma with the group's help. However, David felt that this had not helped him at all. The problem with David was that he could not say about the story of his life: This is my story, I am the hero of this story, and this story has a future. Far from feeling he was the hero of his story, he felt he had played a despicable part. Moreover, there was no future for someone who, having already proved himself a coward, had allowed his stepdaughter to fall to her death. He deserved eternal shame and punishment. Strangest of all, he felt that all these things were happening to someone else. This was not the David he could recognize from his past. Somehow, he had become dislodged from his own life.)

I contacted David and found him in awful shape. He had left the therapy group and was alone and miserable. I told him that I had thought a lot about him when abroad, and had reached the conclusion that he had never had the benefit of a proper military inquiry. He should relate the events that had led to his commander's death and to his falling into captivity to someone in authority who could deliver an official opinion. David said that the only person he could trust with his story was his regiment commander. Anyone unacquainted with the battle would never be able to understand. He gave me the commander's name and I located him. He was still in the army and was now a general. We met and I told him of David's case. I told him that to my mind David judged himself much more harshly than any commission of inquiry would. He remembered David well, was sympathetic and understanding, and agreed to conduct a personal inquiry. David and I received a formal invitation to the central headquarters of the Israeli Army.

The morning of the inquiry, David was acutely anxious. He told me he was not coming, for he simply could not stand the ordeal. I feared that if he refused to come his condition would deteriorate even more. Knowing how much he trusted and needed me, I told him peremptorily that if he did not come I would never treat him again. He gave in.

On our way in, we were checked at a series of gates. At each point, David's name and mine with our full military credentials were already registered. As we came closer to the heart of the headquarters where the general sat, the examinations grew more and more rigorous. We were given magnetic passes to come through the turnstile that led to the innermost chambers. In the final lap we were escorted by the general's orderly. The general received us warmly. The wrinkled original map of the battle, with its faded pencil markings and battle dirt, was pinned to the wall. The general told David that he remembered him well and mentioned other soldiers and officers from David's unit. Soon, however, he became formal and told David, "I am to conduct a commander's inquiry about what happened to you in the war. I was told that you feel very bad about what you did. In order to reach a conclusion, we have to reconstruct all the events in detail. When we are done, I will answer whatever questions you may have. This is the original map of the battle. You can see here the area where your unit was posted. Describe to me where you were and what you did until you fell into captivity."

The first interview lasted two hours. The general asked many questions about what had happened to the tank, which communication net they were in, how David had tried to call for help, and how he had fallen into captivity. David related the events in great detail. The general then adjourned the meeting and invited us again for the next day. I stayed with David for another hour and suggested that he write down all the questions he would like to ask the general. David was deeply moved. He felt the Israeli Army was taking him seriously. Still, he was very much afraid of what the general might say.

Next morning, David arrived with a self-directed bill of indictment which he read to the general: "By allowing my commander to die without being able to call for help, I failed in the most basic duty of a soldier. By bungling the radio connection, I threw the tank and its crew into the hands of the enemy. By falling into captivity without fighting to the end, I disgraced not only my own name, but also yours, sir, and the Israeli Army's."

The general listened carefully to the self-accusation and asked to examine the written page. He told David that there was not one soldier who had fought in the war whose heart was not burdened by guilt. David asked him, respectfully: "Sir, I want to ask you a personal question. Did you ever feel guilt similar to mine?" The general replied: "Ever since the war, not one day goes by without my seeing the horrible picture of the tanks burning with my men inside, or reexperiencing myself in my car over the hill, looking helpelessly at all the horror, or hearing the agonized voices screaming for help through the radio. Everyday I wrack my mind about what I could have done differently. I know full well what it is to feel guilty. Every real soldier is well acquainted with guilt." For minutes, the three of us could not speak.

Then he reread David's charge sheet and said: "Your falling into captivity did not disgrace anyone. There is no ruling in the Israeli Army that one should not fall into captivity. On the contrary, life is our highest value. You are actually blaming yourself for not having died instead of being captured. I tell you—had you died instead of being captured—you would have only caused more suffering and lengthened the roll of the dead in that awful war. We do not believe that suicide is justified in any case. A soldier must care for his life. You did right in saving your own life. No soldier who was taken prisoner was ever accused or tried by the Israeli Army. You are not different from anyone else.

"As for your failure in using the radio. That was not as it should be. Such a failure, however, is not a case of misconduct but of bad soldiering. Had you been better trained, this would not have happened. Your bad soldiering, however, was due to the training that we commanders gave you. Soldiering is the responsibility of the commanders." The general answered all of David's questions in the same vein. He concluded, "In all the points you have raised you cannot be found guilty or even liable for rebuke. I have been told that you have suffered much and that your life is a mess. You have paid dearly enough, even though you have not been found guilty."

I asked the general: "Sir, if we were now in 1974, at the time of David's return from captivity, what would you say to him at the end of your inquiry?" The general replied forthwith: "Get your equipment into the tent and climb onto the tank!"

The general's words had been carefully thought out and delivered with conviction. David was infinitely grateful. The two sessions were tape-recorded and David listened to them many times. He believed in the sincerity of the general's pronouncements and accepted his verdict. David felt he had been rehabilitated and reaccepted into human society. Two weeks after the inquiry, he wrote the following letter to the general:

"Sir:

I want to thank you from the bottom of my heart for giving so generously of your time and attention. In particular, I was moved by your personal warmth. Your sincerity and fatherly behavior eliminated all sense of personal distance. I want, especially, to thank you for speaking your mind truly, without prettifying things. You dared to open old wounds, so as to get to the truth. You helped me tremendously by telling me that it is possible and necessary to go on living, even with the burden of the past. I understood from your words that it was not I who was abnormal but that horrible war. Your words softened somewhat my self-accusations. I hope our interview will also have practical consequences; I want to justify the attention you gave me by being of help to others. To this end I want to take an active part in the Veterans' Association. Devoting myself to the help of suffering veterans will be for me a form of reparation.

"One more request. I would like to participate in the yearly meeting of the regiment's veterans, so that I may feel, once again, part of it. I want you to know that it was a great privilege for me to have fought under your command."

David began to care for his apartment and appearance. He joined the Veterans' Association, participating in gatherings and devoting himself to the help of disabled members. He felt that the guilt over the war had been cleared. He hoped the same might happen with his feelings about the death of his stepdaughter.

Soon, however, another inquiry and trial were to dismantle many of the gains that had been so laboriously achieved. David was charged with forgery (for using the checkbook he had found). Once again he felt himself demoted from his status as a citizen. His paranoid fantasies returned and once again he feared that the Egyptians and the Mossad were after him. His plea that he had never used the checks for his personal use but only for his stepdaughters went unheeded. He was found guilty but was not sent to jail because of my deposition on his condition. The damage, however, was done. David felt rejected by the society into which he had thought himself reintegrated. What followed was a sad and convoluted story of blame and counterblame. He accused the Ministry of Defense of throwing him to the dogs and was accused, in turn, by the ministry's personnel of attempting to squeeze advantages from his psychological condition. After endless tribulation they awarded him the right to an apartment but only on condition that a custodian, acceptable to the ministry, be put in charge. David refused, arguing that this proviso reduced him to the status of second-class citizen. His life had become a legal labyrinth.

All through this period he was much encouraged by a cassette of hypnotherapy, in which I had described his story as a self-imposed life-sentence that had been rendered obsolete and unjustified since the inquiry by his commander. David listened daily to this cassette for almost two years. The commander's inquiry and its elaboration in the hypno-therapeutic narrative gradually helped restore his sense of value.

I am still involved with the case. The issue of the apartment was slowly and agonizingly resolved by compromise. David feels that he has revoked his life-sentence. He stopped taking tranquilizers and is learning to drive. The driving license has become almost emblematic of normal citizen status. He now feels that his role in the war was far from shameful. I recently gave a television interview in which I related David's story. I mentioned that the general had said that at worst David might have displayed flawed soldiership. David was very angry with me for having said so much. "What flawed soldiership are you talking about? I was a hero! Were you there in the tank and in the prisoners' camp to say otherwise?" I was overjoyed by his rebuke. His life has also gained a sense of a future. Now, more than twenty years after the war, we two share the feeling of having possibly found an exit from the labyrinth of justice that is not barred by an impassable guardian.

War Never-ending

Yoram, an industrial manager, in his fifties, was a high-ranking army reserve officer. In the past, he had been in command of one of Israel's special combat units, where he had earned a reputation for conscientiousness and dependability. In the course of one of its missions, his unit fell into an ambush and sustained heavy losses. Yoram was ejected from his command vehicle by a missile hit and lay on the ground for hours until his rescue, badly wounded in his legs and abdomen. The death toll had been ghastly. During his hospital stay, bad news about the wounded, the missing, and the dead kept filtering in. In spite of the many years that had passed since then, Yoram described these events to me in a state of acute agitation.

Yoram told me that when the strategic principles for the deployment of his unit had been formulated, he had insisted on security measures which would, in all probability, have prevented the catastrophe. Some of Yoram's proposals were rejected because they involved expensive equipment. Yoram felt that even those that were accepted had been negligently implemented. He complained to the authorities, but his pleas went unheeded. After a while he gave in and let matters stand as they were. After the disastrous battle, he blamed himself bitterly for his docility and lack of perseverance.

In spite of his agitation, Yoram described in great detail all that had befallen him and his unit: how they had distanced themselves from the rest of the troops; the awful moment when they had found themselves under heavy fire; the shock of the anti-tank missile on his vehicle; the bad state of his legs and abdomen; the burning vehicles and the bodies on the ground; the helplessness, the partial reorganization, and the final rescue of the survivors. The tale was far from chaotic. Yoram gave the impression that he could peruse the killing field almost at will, picking up on any detail or sequence of events. The whole scene seemed to be fully available and transparent to his mind.

He told also of the disappointment he had experienced when he realized that there would be no serious inquiry about the causes of the disaster. The formal investigation was being pursued in a desultory manner. His queries were met with evasive replies: whitewashing seemed to have become official policy. After leaving the hospital and later the army, Yoram tried again and again to resuscitate the inquiry. This activity was viewed with growing disaffection by the people in charge. He tried to pursue the investigation on his own, but was denied access to the archives. Even those who had not been involved in the original decisional process viewed Yoram's attempts to dig up the matter as unjustified. Yoram's unit had not been the only one to sustain heavy losses and the official commission of inquiry had, in their view, done its job. Yoram seemed to be involved in a private war of self-justification. Faced with massive opposition, Yoram once again gave in.

(True, Yoram needed the investigation for personal reasons as well. Without it, his life story would remain an open wound. He who had always taken pride in his conscientiousness had become guilty of fatal negligence. He could not recognize himself in this story, much less view himself as any kind of hero. His only hope for a redeeming change lay in starting up an investigation that would prevent similar mistakes in the future. This option might restore a sense of purpose to his existence.)

Yoram had all the symptoms associated with post-traumatic stress disorder: sleep disturbances, nightmares, irritability, emotional outbursts, disrupted personal relationships, intrusive flashbacks, depression, and most of all, an excruciating sense of guilt. One blatant manifestation of his sense of guilt was his inability to converse, socialize or even stay in the same room with the parents of fallen soldiers. He had once abandoned a therapy group in which he felt he was helped when he found out that one of the participants was a bereaved parent. On another occasion he had left a promising job for the same reason. His acute sense of guilt became manifest also in more roundabout ways. For instance, any shadow of neglect in the maintenance of equipment or in the implementation of safety rules would drive him into a fury, unless the people concerned corrected their oversights immediately. These angry outbursts had made him leave one managerial position after another.

When Yoram first came to me, he had just been accepted as a manager by a construction firm. One of the first duties he took upon himself was to compose a safety manual for the workers. He showed me the manual, a brochure bristling with graphs and tables that would satisfy the strictest pedant. Drawing graphs and tabling data seemed to provide Yoram with a sense of control. I proposed that we should begin our work together by helping him deal with his difficulties at work by a judicious use of this skill. His first task would be to monitor and table his weekly mood changes.

(The occupational problem was chosen as a starting point because whereas the war experience was relatively continuous and well-organized, the interface between war and work was far from smooth. It was as if Yoram were saying: someone with a war story like mine cannot go on working as if nothing had happened. Thus, in choosing to focus on work, the therapist was not laying the traumatic experience aside. On the contrary, he was addressing the trauma at the precise point where it was causing the most acute discontinuity in the narrative.)

Yoram arrived at the following session with a neat and multicolored graph representing his ups and downs during the week. So there were good moments, too! Yoram was very satisfied. Attending to the graph had distracted him for a while from his sufferings. With the help of the graph, we started to pinpoint the triggers of his irritation; they invariably had to do with neglect. He had discovered to his dismay that others, even the owners of the firm, were quite indifferent to the maintenance of equipment, to say nothing of the personal security of the workers. In the past such a discovery would surely have made him leave his job. Yoram agreed that this was a very ineffective response, and one that caused him and his family endless damage. However, he would only agree to stay on the job if he had good grounds to believe that he could remedy the neglect. To achieve this end, I became Yoram's organizational consultant. Together, we searched for more effective ways whereby Yoram might have his opinions heard. He learned to bide his time, express his position acceptably, muster alliances, and take into consideration the interests of others. Each success was a partial corrective for his past failings. He would no longer give in on vital matters, nor would he leave the field. He gradually succeeded in making important changes in the firm's care of equipment and safety regulations.

Gradually he grew confident enough to approach the military with a new plan for an independent inquiry. This time he went about his job differently. He began by a series of preparatory contacts. He readied himself for setbacks and planned in advance for tactical retreats. And in spite of considerable opposition, he gained access to the crucial archives.

His wife Nira was among those who were opposed to Yoram's concern with the past. She thought that it only aggravated his condition. Yoram should concentrate on the present and bury the past. Gradually his almost obsessive pursuit and her profound disaffection with it created a severe strain in their relationship. The trauma was severing him from his wife.

I thought that a few marital sessions might help to bridge the gap. It was not to be so. Faced with Nira's decided refusal to listen to his arguments in favor of the inquiry, Yoram lost control and started to scream. He even lifted a chair, as if to smash it on her head. One of my neighbors, an army officer himself, was frightened by the noise and ran into my garden, gun in hand. Only when, peeping through the window, he saw me sitting safe and sound, and the attacker gradually calming down, did he slouch silently back to his home. Nira addressed me angrily, saying that ever since I had decided to support Yoram in his digging up of the past, his mood had deteriorated and he was less and less involved with her and with their sons. I was struck dumb by her vehemency. The session ended on a very bad note. Fortunately Yoram gradually began to deal more constructively with some of Nira's complaints. He became closer to his sons, first of all by telling them his story in great detail. He devoted more time and attention to Nira, and in time, she mollified somewhat. However, Yoram understood that his hopes of sharing his major preoccupation with her were unrealistic.

In spite of the improvement at work and the promising new start of Yoram's inquiry, the trauma's affective presence in Yoram's life was not much reduced. He was still plagued by recurrent bouts of depression and was unable to participate in public events connected with his unit. He repeatedly refused to give interviews and lectures that might have strengthened his position and helped his inquiry. He knew that he would have to do so; otherwise the impact of the inquiry would be badly restricted. However, the very thought that a bereaved relative might be in the audience paralyzed him. His moods would become particularly black around anniversary dates connected with the war. At those times it would seem as if we were back to square one. Yoram would be haunted by flashbacks and nightmares, become obsessed with guilt, lose control over his anger, and retreat into his dark shell. At this juncture, after more than six months of therapy, I offered to deal directly with the war experience.

I told Yoram that in my experience people often succeeded in dealing with their traumata on their own, if life conditions improved enough to allow them to do so. This, however, had not happened in his case. In spite of the improvement in daily functioning and of the fact that he now had a positive goal that gave meaning to his life, the war experience continued to plague him. I offered to conduct a series of ten extended sessions, in which Yoram would be required to face the war memories directly. The sessions would take place at night, after we had both finished our daily obligations, so that we might stay for as long as needed. We spaced the sessions over three weeks. We would start with a relaxation exercise, following which I would ask Yoram to visualize the events of the battle, focusing on each painful act, thought, and feeling. I told him that we would not interrupt the visualization until the images had become bearable to him, either on account of habituation or of mental exhaustion. He might start, for instance, by focusing on the body of a dead soldier lying in the field. I would then ask him to say the worst things that came to his mind. He would say he was responsible for the soldier's death; that he owed the soldier's parents his life; that they had trusted him with their son and that he had betrayed their charge; that he had left the soldier's wife a widow and his 2-year-old child an orphan. When he could no longer talk, I would tell him to relax and then to start again. Little by little, he learned to bear the frightful images. He had viewed again and again the shower of missiles coming upon him and his men. He had been present in imagination at each of his soldiers' burial ceremonies. He talked to each bereaved parent, widow, and orphan. He expressed for the first time, his own anguish and fear for his own death and his pain at parting from his wife and kids. At the end of one of the sessions, Yoram found an appropriate name for the procedure: *The Inquisition.*

(The choice of the name points to the relationship between work on the trauma and on the life narrative. The procedure involved not only the trauma's abreaction, but also a rite of expiation. Yoram's sufferings in the sessions were highly relevant in this respect: they were the guilty offerings of the sinner to the inner tribunal of his conscience. The historical Inquisition tortured the sinner and exacted confession, but also gave absolution. Like a repentant sinner, Yoram seemed to be asking for the appropriate penance to relieve his guilt. This consideration explained the direct, almost cruel way

the trauma was being processed. The therapist who, when working with other clients with traumatic conditions would usually opt either for avoiding any direct traumatic work or for a very gradual and mild approach, found himself donning the cloak of the great inquisitor. The stakes, however, were high. If successful, the experience might restore Yoram to the human community from which he had cut himself off in his guilt and shame.)

The effects of the inquisition were clear-cut. One week after its conclusion, Yoram gave his first interview on the radio. In the following month, he gave a lecture about his unit and the fateful battle before an audience of cadets. The interest he aroused led to his lecture becoming a fixture in various advanced army courses. He started to appear on television. He saw his public appearances as a corrective experience. He taught the cadets, officers, and public a critical attitude that would oppose all whitewashing. He had come out of the dark chambers of the inquisition imbued with a sense of mission.

(The reconstructed narrative of Yoram's life made good sense to him now. He could recognize himself as the sinner who was trying to make good on his transgressions by public corrective acts. He was a hero with a flaw, but still a hero, and he had a goal and a mission, almost prophetic in scope.)

The treatment went on for a few additional months. Yoram's inquiry and his fight with the military censorship to publish its results took more than ten years. We have recently met, Nira, Yoram, and I, to celebrate with a meal and champagne the publication of his almost unexpurgated book.

6

A NARRATIVE ATTITUDE TO PSYCHOTHERAPY

Perhaps the chief problem with any set of principles of narrative reconstruction is that there are so many of them; even our sprawling list is at best only a small and biased selection. How can the therapist be expected to keep so many things in mind? If before each and every utterance the therapist were to worry about characterization, plots, themes, and meanings, she would probably choose to remain silent. A possible solution to this taxing complexity, which has been utilized by various psychotherapeutic approaches, is to define a generalized frame of mind or a therapeutic attitude that simplifies and epitomizes the approach's outlook on the nature of problems and the process of change. The narrative view, although not a full-fledged therapeutic approach with its own specific theory, methodology, and technique, may offer precisely such a therapeutic attitude, which may help to modulate the therapist's favored approach. It would then be possible for a psychoanalytic, humanist, systemic, or cognitive therapist to work narratively within the framework of her own approach. The new narratives they would help to create would naturally be colored by their own theoretical inclinations. Whatever the inclination however we believe that the better therapists are those who help their clients develop better narratives. We also believe that a narrative attitude would increase the possibilities for developing a superior therapeutic narrative.

What would then constitute the basis of the narrative attitude? How could we epitomize it, so the therapist might cultivate it? To our minds, the two central ideas that summarize the narrative attitude as we have put forth in this book are those of narrative empathy and therapeutic splitting. In our view all the principles we have enunciated regarding characterization, plots, themes, and meanings can be compressed into these two basic notions and be unfolded from them.

Narrative empathy as we have described it refers to the therapist's attempt to make sense of the client's behavior, uncover its inner logic and offer her a resonant emotional response. The empathy is achieved through the narrative: the therapist builds together with the client a story that credits the client as having developed a reasonable solution to the harsh conditions in which she found herself.

Therapeutic splitting stresses the therapist's consideration of both the negative and the positive sides of the client's responses. The assumption underlying this concept is that any pattern of behavior brought to therapy as a problem represents both an achievement and a failure. We believe that the attempt to talk only about effective solutions and positive outcomes slights the price and the pain that are being exacted. Conversely, any exclusive focus on the negative, the irrational, and the immature, slights the client's efforts and achievements.

The attitude that is epitomized by narrative empathy and therapeutic splitting may provide us with an answer to some controversial issues regarding the therapist's position. It may, for instance, offer a viable answer to the problem of deceitful manipulation. Deceit and its passive cousin, the witholding of information, may result from our distrust that the client can make good use of our knowledge or opinions. Indeed, if we think of the client in negative, pathological, or hopeless terms, or in any way we know the client would be sure to reject, we are almost driven to some measure of deceit. Alternatively, deceit sometimes results from strategic considerations; the therapist then utilizes the client's responses as a lever to change, without disclosing his plans. Narrative empathy and therapeutic splitting may help us avoid these undesirable options. Thus, through a constant effort at narrative empathy, the therapist can reach an understanding of the client's unusual patterns that, far from pejorative, is perfectly acceptable to the client. Furthermore, through therapeutic splitting, instead of utilizing the problematic aspects of the client's behavior underhandedly, the therapist may include them explicitly in the therapeutic narrative. Instead of paradoxically encouraging a symptomatic pattern, the therapist may underline the positive aspects of the pattern (insofar as it reflects a real achievement or an understandable solution to an impossible situation), while also presenting in straightforward terms the pain and the damage it involves. In our experience this cards-on-the-table policy, far from wasting the strategic advantages of indirect or paradoxical approaches, transmutes them into the stuff of a frank and warm therapeutic alliance.

Narrative empathy and therapeutic splitting also offer us an alternative either to therapeutic confrontation or to a bland attitude of unconditional support. Therapists often feel the need to present their clients with unpalatable truths. Ever since its inception, psychotherapy has viewed itself as a procedure for unearthing and unmasking painful and shameful psychic material. Traumata, secrets, evasions, double-dealings, and hidden drives are some of the dark recesses we often feel our mission to expose. We all know, however, how ineffective or damaging an unsympathetic confrontation can be. Clients often reject the putative truths we confront them with or, perhaps even worse, accept them. Still, we feel obliged to disclose them under pain of feeling disloyal to our calling. The narrative attitude offers a solution to this dilemma. No raw truths must be hurled at the client; on the contrary, any new understanding must be first distilled so as to make perfect human sense to therapist and client alike. This is the basic requirement of narrative empathy. Unless the putative truth be made fully acceptable so that the client may take it to heart with no loss of self-respect, it cannot be deemed therapeutic. The objection might perhaps be raised that such a strictly protective stance toward the client would lead to an anemic therapy, a saccharinic endeavor, all stroke and little push. Therapeutic splitting obviates this danger. The therapist has already shown herself to be on the client's side with the positive prong of the split, and she can now express herself with the harshness she may feel necessary. Needless to say, both sides of the split must pass the test of narrative empathy, and the client must be able to recognize himself fully in the description. The positive, however, must temper the negative and open the way to its acceptance.

The combination of positive and negative tones in the therapeutic split makes for a rounded narrative. It modulates the triumphant optimism (excessive to our taste), that sometimes prevails with constructive therapists. We would like therapy to span the full range of human emotion: compromise, failure, and suffering are not only part of the problem but also part of the solution. The therapeutic vocabulary of progress must leave a place for resignation as well as for triumph.

We contend that a narrative perspective can fit with one's affiliation to any therapeutic orientation. We can have psychoanalytic, cognitive, systemic, and humanist narrative therapists. The narrative angle surely modifies the therapist's relationship to his underlying approach, for its propositions are no longer viewed as objective truths but as provisional ways of organizing the therapeutic material. We might go as far as to say that the best moments of therapy are those in which we and our clients discover the limitations and biases of our own provisional descriptions. Therapy reaches its highest points by self-transcendence, by therapist and client alike.

Consider an impasse situation: the therapist has labored to achieve a description of the client and her problem that may open avenues for change. However, the client cannot or will not make use of this description. Therapy becomes stalemated. Its strategies grind to a halt. The therapeutic relationship suffers. It was once widely believed that these were obligatory crises indicating the area and extent of the client's resistance, and that therapy would have to overcome this resistance in order to progress. The narrative perspective does not eliminate these crises but their expected solution is different. Impasse situations are occasions for re-narration. They are pointers to the limitations in our descriptions. They may be solved if the therapist (and not only the client) succeeds in overcoming his own resistance and in modifying his provisional narratives so as to make better sense to the client (Omer 1994).

The narrative attitude aims constantly at such self-transcendence. Ideally, therapists should always view their narratives as calling for empathic enlargement, as lacking in some dimension that might offer our clients more room for self-recognition, for a central role, and for significant options. We should always be intent on extending our capacity for encompassing newer and stranger personal experiences, rendering them transparent to our minds, vibrating with them, making them our own. The great Belgian writer Marguerite Yourcenar, in her *Memoirs of Hadrian*, construed the figure of her wise Roman emperor as a man bent on extending his capacity to understand what is different, on integrating into himself ever more foreign ways of thinking and experiencing, on stretching the limits of his self by bringing in the strange and the alien. His position as emperor was the very embodiment of this personal task. He considered it his duty to embrace within his inner empire the otherness of even the most exotic of his subjects. He did not even stop with humanity, but pushed his own limits to feel the motions of his horse, and the mutual touch of the swimmer and the water. His efforts at self-transcendence reached to the very limit of life: he would attempt to make out, without supernatural adjunctions, the very profile of his death. Hadrian embodies not only the ideal of the emperor, but also of the novelist, who puts herself at the cutting edge of human experience, enlarging its boundaries by additional characters, new lives, and fresh perceptions. It is in this noble lineage and with the help of the narrative perspective that we hope to place ourselves as therapists. Not in our achievements, but in our true desire.

7

HISTORICAL FOUNDATIONS OF THE NARRATIVE APPROACH

In the course of the last thirty years, the basic assumptions shared by the major schools of psychotherapy concerning the nature of mental disturbance and its cure, the status of clinical and empirical evidence, and the position of psychotherapeutic theories, have changed. It was commonly assumed that mental disorder was a natural phenomenon with objective existence; that it was due to real causes both necessary and sufficient; that the process of cure began with the correct diagnosis of the disorder and its causes (both past and present) and ended when these causes were eliminated; that there was one fundamental level to which all explanations in psychotherapy could be reduced; that only one theory could be correct, for only one theory could present a mirror image of reality; that only one method of exploration and validation was correct and scientific; that only one cure, the one that reversed the pathogenic process, was real; and that only by basing itself on these assumptions could psychotherapy constitute itself as a fully scientific discipline and earn a place in the edifice of established knowledge.

These assumptions reflect the positivist world view. Positivism was not just one philosophy among others. It was the most ambitious, inclusive, and enduring program of knowledge in the Western world since the end of the Middle Ages. It set up scientific knowledge as the model for all human knowledge, the scientific method as the touchstone of human rationality, and a scientifically based world as the promised land for those who followed its precepts. Those who refused to accept the privileged standing of the scientific method and its findings were relegated to the status of obscurantists, irrationalists, superstition mongers, and charlatans. The scientific method was one, and so was scientific truth. Free from the vagaries of human judgment and its limited perspectives, scientific knowledge was unshakable. It was the modern counterpart of *God's point of view*, displaying things as they really were. No discipline in the intellectual arena could hope for influence without subscribing to the precepts of science, making use of its vocabulary, or donning its mantle. Modern psychotherapy could never have risen but as a scientific endeavor.

In the course of the last thirty years, however, these assumptions have been radically shaken. The once solid world of psychotherapy in which there was room for only one reality, one theory, one method, and one cure fragmented into a multiple relativism, in a process that we shall term *the pluralist revolution*. This change was not peculiar to psychotherapy. Indeed, in the last few decades, the positivist monolith has been buffeted by critical blasts from many directions. These onslaughts have performed their erosive work, often without any mutual awareness. To use a historical analogy, the positivistic edifice may be likened to the Roman Empire of human knowledge, and the anti-positivist attacks to barbarian forays (no offense meant to the anti-positivists) arriving pell-mell at many places and at different times. Each barbarian tribe had no idea that it was part of the "barbarian invasions." The positivist giant often felt little pressure from the skirmishes at the borders. Their cumulative effects, however, slowly began to make a difference. Anti-positivism became more organized, the positivist defense became more strenuous and less effective, many positivists became barbarized and many barbarians positivized. Positivism did not disappear but went on existing alongside other world views, sometimes even staging a local reaction. The pluralist revolution in psychotherapy can be viewed as a stage in this cultural drama and we shall try to sketch its course. Without this background, the principles of narrative reconstruction already described would make little sense.

THE DECLINE OF PSYCHOPATHOLOGICAL REALISM

In its strictest form, psychopathological realism holds the view that mental disorder is an illness that resides deep within the client's mind or brain and underlies symptomatology. The very term *symptom* underscores the belief that the manifest problem is not the real one. Diagnosis is the process of discovery and identification of the underlying illness. In this perspective, mental or behavioral problems are viewed as real things that are ensconced in real places and should not be superficially tampered with. Attempts at mere symptom removal should therefore be viewed as naïve and irresponsible.

The pluralist revolution witnessed and was instrumental in bringing about a radically new understanding, according to which mental problems owe their being to the *language games*[1] through which human reality is construed. Examples of these games are: labeling, categorizing, telling and enacting stories, giving and receiving unwitting suggestions, arousing and fulfilling expectations. By their diagnostic and curative efforts, therapists become active participants in these games, helping at times to maintain the very reality they are bent on eradicating.

The passage from strict psychopathological realism into this linguistic perspective did not come about in one leap. It was a many-staged process, and ironically some of its instigators, the behavior therapists, were devoted positivists. For their positivist sin they are often viewed as arch-reactionaries, even by many who unwittingly repeat their original ideas. The early behaviorists, for instance, were the first to uncover the conceptual weaknesses and the therapeutic dangers

1. The term *language games* is derived from Wittgenstein (1958). It refers to the philosophical thesis according to which, by means of language, we construe our world, to which we often tend to attribute an independent reality.

inherent in the application of the *medical model* to behavioral problems. One of their seminal contributions, their rejection of the widespread belief in symptom substitution, stemmed directly from their critique of medical reification. They were also the first to underline the importance of social norms and context in labeling a piece of behavior as symptomatic or pathological (Bandura 1969, Bandura and Walters 1959). For all their innovations the behavior therapists were uncompromising realists. Behavioral disturbances for them were objective phenomena that could be scientifically defined and measured. The locus of pathology had been shifted, but its realist, objective, and deterministic nature had remained. A deeper change was needed and more daring prophets to harbinger it.

Ervin Goffman

Starting with the concept of *total institution*, Goffman (1961) set out to show how social labeling and cultural bracketing create mental walls that are often no less thick and rigid than the concrete walls of the prisons and mental hospitals from which he culled his descriptions. Without arguing directly with the putative reality of mental illness, Goffman's critique considerably weakened psychopathological realism, since much of what is usually attributed to mental illness can be explained by the social interactions that develop once such a concept is put to use. For example, Goffman argues that the very concept of mental illness gives rise to a veritable *mental patient career*, in the course of which an individual's relationship to the world at large, significant others, and self are molded anew. Let us take a closer look at Goffman's analysis.

The career is launched by the events leading to hospitalization. Hospitalization, a crucial event that influences the whole course of the disturbance, follows from the concept of mental illness, for otherwise there would be little reason to choose a hospital rather than a prison, a holiday resort, or simply a period of home rest. The decision to hospitalize is, furthermore, never just a function of the symptoms. Numerous contingencies play a role. The family situation, for instance, is often crucial. An elderly parent may be kept at home until his adult children move from a house into an apartment; an adolescent's rebellion may be tolerated until she starts an affair with a married man; and a depressed husband may become unbearable once the wife finds herself a lover. A queer illness, Goffman implies, whose course can be so much affected by contingencies.

Little by little, small fissures in the interpersonal world of the patient-to-be grow into veritable chasms. Consider the next-of-kin, who usually plays a crucial role in the process of hospitalization. The candidate for hospitalization is not often told that the next-of-kin has already talked to the doctor and described the symptoms. In the interview at the clinic, the doctor usually speaks differently to her than to the next-of-kin, establishing a coalition of normals. When hospitalization ensues, there is an inevitable feeling of abandonment often reinforced by the next-of-kin's visits. The patient (for now she is officially one) may then beg for an early release or at least for privileges that would make life in the institution more bearable, while the relative, no matter how pained or remorseful, is led either to ignore the requests or to claim that all is being done for her good. When the family member nonchalantly leaves for the external world, now viewed by the inmate as thick with bounties, a sense of betrayal must ensue. Declarations of sympathy are often perceived as no more than a pious gloss. Perhaps even more important than the betrayal, however, is the fact that the patient starts to feel that the gap between his present life and previous normal life is growing so wide as to become almost unbridgeable.

This estrangement from family or from other representatives of the quickly crystallizing outside world deepens at each stage of the passage from person to patient. Thus, the diagnosing doctor may receive the patient-to-be in a plush suite, displaying interest and courtesy, an attitude that is quickly belied by what is to follow. Similarly, the staff members who are charged with conveying her to the hospital may show a friendly attitude, joking with her and offering her cigarettes, as if they had nothing to do with the confinement. Alienation and exclusion grow apace.

In the official act of hospitalization, the patient is deprived of many of the signs and attributes that usually constitute personal identity. The freedom to choose where and when to eat, to relax, to retreat to one's privacy, and whom to meet or avoid meeting, is revoked. Practically, all interactions involving social recognition by which the person was defined as carpenter, teacher, philanthropist, or housewife are abolished in a veritable process of *role dispossession*. Personal objects and articles of clothing, termed the *identity kit* by Goffman, are often consigned with the management upon arrival. The process of depersonalization is pursued in the staff's relationship to inmates. Patients are usually talked about, labeled, and discussed, as if they were absent. The management of large numbers of people requires that the chief role of staff with inmates be one of surveillance, rather than guidance. A mutual fit must develop between staff and patients so as to allow for the institution's smooth functioning. This process is abetted by the formation of stereotypes and rigid norms of relating. Staff are led to view inmates as secretive, untrustworthy, and weak, while inmates now view staff as condescending, highhanded, and mean. Social distance is very pronounced: even talk across boundaries may be conducted in a special tone of voice. Information is compartmentalized, and inmates develop their own clandestine world while staff members share knowledge of discreditable information about inmates. As they adapt to the world of the hospital, patients necessarily lose their acculturation to the world outside. The passage from the one to the other, particularly when one has succeeded in attaining some status in the ward and must enter the outside world from the bottom, becomes fraught with dangers.

Identity change is insidiously furthered by the development of new biographies. One particularly insidious rewrite of the life-story begins with the admission interview, goes on through the official record of hospitalization, and reaches its final form in the case-report. Patients are gradually led to accept the truth and objectivity of the case-report. The achievement of such insight not only improves the chances of release but also helps patients to conceive of their relatives as decent persons rather than as persecutors.

This new version, however, highlights precisely those events that in other circumstances people would choose to conceal. The self that emerges from these transactions must therefore be endowed with a rather thick rind of protective shamelessness.

The cumulative effect of Goffman's description is deeper and more lasting than the initial moral indignation that it arouses. In a transformation parallel to the one undergone by the inmate's identity, we gradually come to see mental illness as a result, no less than as a cause, of the labels, the innuendos, the rules, the secrets—in short, of the language games that surround it. If we ever conceived of language games as playful, Goffman's work (1961) will certainly disabuse us.

Ronald Laing

A standard allegation of the anti-psychiatric movement against psychiatrists is that they turn persons into objects or passive organisms to be classified, organized, observed, and molded. In Laing's writings these almost trivial claims become far more than mere protest slogans. Rather than being inherently inhumane, psychiatrists in his view are themselves the dupes of a vocabulary that depicts the individual as a self-contained entity to be understood without reference to its relational world (Laing 1959). Schizophrenia, for instance, is defined by its symptoms, irrespective of the context in which these symptoms are manifested. The diagnosing context is naïvely assumed to add nothing to the entity being diagnosed.

Laing argues that the context is constitutive of the person as much as the person, of the context. The act of observation affects its object as much as the object affects the observation. The moment the person is looked at or asked a question, his world is ineluctably affected. This is cogently illustrated in Laing's analysis of one of Kraepelin's cases. Here is Kraepelin:

> The patient I will show you today has almost to be carried into the rooms, as he walks in a straddling fashion on the outside of his feet. On coming in, he throws off his slippers, sings a hymn loudly, and then cries twice (in English), "My father, my real father!" He is eighteen years old . . . [He] sits with his eyes shut, and pays no attention to his surroundings. He does not look up even when he is spoken to . . . he answers beginning in a low voice, and gradually screaming louder and louder. When asked where he is, he says, "You want to know that too? I tell you who is being measured and is measured and shall be measured. I know all that, and could tell you, but I do not want to." When asked his name, he screams, "What is your name? What does he shut? He shuts his eyes. What does he hear? He does not understand; he understands not. How? Who? Where? When? What does he mean? When I tell him to look he does not look properly. You there, just look! What is it? What is the matter? Attend; he attends not. I say, what is it, then? Why do you give me no answer? Are you getting impudent again? How can you be so impudent? I'm coming! I'll show you! You don't whore for me. You mustn't be smart either; you're an impudent, lousy fellow, such an impudent, lousy fellow I've never met with. Is he beginning again? You understand nothing at all, nothing at all; nothing at all does he understand" . . . and so on. At the end, he scolds in quite inarticulate sounds [Kraepelin 1905, pp. 79–80].

Kraepelin goes on to comment on the inaccessibility of this patient. "He has not given us a single piece of useful information. His talk was . . . only a series of disconnected sentences having no relation whatever to the general situation" (p. 80). "The signs," continues Kraepelin, "are obviously those of catatonic excitement."

Laing does not argue with these signs. Kraepelin, however, has *chosen* to attend to these signs rather than to other aspects of the interaction. He insists on viewing the patient as an observed datum, whereas he, the observer, is not part of the observation. Kraepelin's choice leads to his effecting a diagnosis, but also to his missing the client' s meaning. Laing guides our attention to Kraepelin himself, the would-be uninvolved observer, so that we may view him as an unwittingly involved participant. The patient seems to be carrying on a dialogue between his own version of Kraepelin and himself. One might be tempted to rewrite the patient's productions in dialogue form.

Kraepelin: I tell you who is being measured and is measured and shall be measured.

Patient: I know all you ask me and could tell you, but I do not want to.

Kraepelin: What is your name? (To the students) He does not understand . . . When I tell him to look he does not look properly. (To the client again) You there, just look! . . . Why do you give me no answer? Are you getting impudent again? You don't whore for me (prostitute yourself in front of the audience)!

In this redescription the patient is no longer an isolated object of observation but an interacting person who includes Kraepelin in his own living field.

Another example by Laing of this inclusion of the other in the person's self-experience is provided by an adolescent girl who was diagnosed as suffering from schizophrenia simplex. She was continuously involved in the inner contemplation of a game of tennis (mixed doubles) in which she figured as the ball. The girl's family consisted of mother, father, mother's father, and father's mother, all living under the same roof. The girl's father and his mother were ranged against the girl's mother and her father (mixed doubles). The two sides often broke off all communication, using the girl as go-between. Her mother would say, "Tell your father to pass the salt," and the daughter would convey the request. The father might then answer, "Tell your mother to get it herself," and the girl would relay the answer. No wonder she experienced herself as a tennis ball (Laing 1971).

These clinical examples illustrate Laing's talent for rescuing clients from the attribution of an inferior objectified status. Their bizarre behaviors can then be understood as attempts to reclaim the self. By their inclusion of others in their own self-descriptions, they become veritable existential rebels who encompass their encompassers, turning the latters' superior gaze into one more viewpoint within their own richer tableau. Mental disease, the objective thing, becomes a game of mutual reflections.

Thomas Szasz

The concept of mental illness, in Szasz's view (1961), is an unworkable hybrid, for the realms of the body obey strictly physical laws, while those of the mind follow language games and interactional rules. Saying that a mental phenomenon is an illness is a category mistake. Szasz does not argue that mind and body are two independent entities. His argument is epistemological: mental phenomena are explained and understood in radically different ways from physical ones. Thus, a Shakespearean play cannot be understood in terms of cortex, limbic system, neurons, and pathways, but only in terms of language, form, imagery, and feelings. Similarly, the behavior of a so-called mental patient has nothing to do with symptoms, illness, and diagnosis, but with messages, communication, symbolization, and control.

The contention that mental illness is a myth or a category mistake has been deemed simplistic by Szasz's critics (e.g., Halgin and Whitbourne 1993). In their opinion, Szasz ignores the overwhelming evidence of genetic factors in psychiatric conditions, the powerful effects of psychiatric drugs, and the findings on abnormal functioning of neurotransmitters. Szasz's attempt to dismiss the whole of organic psychiatry with a semantic shrug is, in their opinion, preposterous.

We shall fail to understand Szasz's arguments, however, if we take it as applying to the concept of brain disease. Szasz has nothing against the bona fide nature of neurological conditions such as epilepsy or Korsakoff's disease. He denies, however, that schizophrenia and depression have been proven to be such. If a physiological test were developed, providing an unequivocal answer to the diagnosis of a schizophrenic brain disease, Szasz would bow to the verdict (which, however, he deems highly unlikely). That no such test exists is clear to him from the fact that even if someone is diagnosed with schizophrenia, there is no accepted procedure (as there is, for epilepsy), by which he can prove incontrovertibly that the diagnosis is wrong. Indeed, in Rosenhan's (1973) classic paper "On Being Sane in Insane Places," all of the eight pseudopatients who got themselves admitted to mental hospitals by claiming they heard voices, were eventually released with a diagnosis of schizophrenia in remission. This was in spite of the fact that, once hospitalized, they displayed absolutely no symptomatic behavior. If not for the preexisting protocols demonstrating these pseudopatients to have faked their symptoms, presumably no power on earth could have disproved their diagnosis. This is an example of a self-fulfilling prophecy; once someone is diagnosed as a schizophrenic, she will remain so for the diagnosis affects the future behavior of doctors and patients alike. Self-fulfilling prophecies are phenomena that characterize the realms of meaning, language, and human communication, not the realms of physics.

Szasz's critique applies best for mental illnesses that are uniformly viewed as inorganic, rather than those suspected to be due to brain dysfunction. Actually, for the latter, we might no longer need the concept of mental illness at all: once demonstrated as physiological, they should be recategorized as bodily illnesses. Szasz's arguments, therefore, become clearest in hysteria, which by definition is not a bodily illness. Defining hysteria as a mental illness involves one in a series of language games that are linked to the concept of *illness*. Thus, one is led to divide the phenomena of hysteria into *symptoms* and *pathogenes*. The category of *pathogenes* is conceptualized in terms such as *energies*, *blocked libido*, *bound cathexes*, and their like; *symptom formation* is viewed as a process of *energy conversion*, and *cure* as one of *energy release*. This terminology is obviously borrowed. What do we actually witness in hysteric behavior? Somebody behaves as if he were ill without being demonstrably so. Obviously, others are a part of this demonstration, for we can hardly conceive of hysteria without an audience (a strange qualification for an illness). Indeed, the hysteric's behavior might be better understood as an attempt (albeit conflicted and unconscious) at influence. The relevant questions are then, whom, how, and why is he trying to influence?

Consider, moreover, the psychiatric attitude towards malingering. As opposed to hysteria, malingering is a conscious faking of bodily illness. When psychiatrists were busy demonstrating the legitimacy of hysteria as an illness, malingering clearly did not qualify as one. Hysteria, the true currency, had to be carefully differentiated from malingering, the counterfeit. Later, when the concept of mental illness had caught on and hysteria figured as one of its distinguished representatives, malingering slowly came to be viewed as a mental illness in its own right. The counterfeit had become a masterpiece too! This process, whereby behavioral problems are systematically brought into the fold of psychiatry, is termed by Szasz *psychoimperialism*. This illustrates for him the kind of expanding muddle into which we must sink if we keep the concept of mental illness.

Michel Foucault

Foucault's *genealogical approach* to the problem of mental illness focuses on the history, or rather the archaeology of the attitude to madness in the Western world, revealing the arbitrary processes by which we came to believe what we believe. In Foucault's (1965/1988) reading, the seventeenth century was a watershed in the history of madness. In the course of a few decades all over Europe, the mad, who had been commonly allowed to wander freely, were confined and banished from humankind. The *great confinement*, as Foucault describes it, made madness totally alien and inaccessible. The language of psychiatry is heir to this attitude; it is not a dialogue *with* the mad, but a monologue of reason and science *about* madness.

Before the great confinement, Foucault argues, madness and the mad were viewed as repositories of secret and forbidden truths and as figures of passion and pain who signaled our own possibilities of transformation. Madness aroused revulsion, but also temptation and awe. The age of reason, which walled in the mad, also walled in its own mind to the intimations of madness. Madness became the anti-human, the absolute other.

The earlier openness to madness did not necessarily involve a uniformly humane attitude toward the afflicted individuals. The mad were often incarcerated, flogged, mocked, and banished. Ship owners, who were sometimes paid to rid a town or county of them, would sail from harbor to harbor, packing the mad in their ships. This was the origin of the half-mythical *Ship of Fools*. Until the great confinement, however, there was no systematic policy of isolation. Persecution was counterbalanced by charity, curiosity, and wonder. Far from being stereotyped as a single horror-inspiring figure, madness had infinite faces: "I count as many images [of madness] as there are men. . . . So many forms of madness abound . . . and each day sees so many new ones born, that a thousand Democrituses would not suffice to mock them" (Erasmus, *In Praise of Folly*, quoted in Foucault [1965/1988], p. 26). This open attitude was based on the belief that folly and sanity coexist within us. The dialogue with madness was thus internal as well as external.

The Age of Reason created an irrevocable split between rationality and irrationality: reason defined the human, non-reason the bestial. Madness was equated with animality; the mad were *monsters* (etymologically, things to be shown). Occasionally, they were trained by their wardens to perform stunning antics for the diversion of a paying audience. The identification of the mad with beasts was also evident in the manner of their keeping—behind bars, chained to walls, often naked. Their feces would be raked through an opening in the grating. Their beastly hide, it was assumed, inured them to crowding, cold, and pain.

The next step in Foucault's argument is perhaps the most controversial. The reforms instituted by Pinel and Tuke, far from liberating and humanizing the mad, were in his view only another link in the chain of their subjugation and objectification. Foucault's concern is not with physical cruelty as such, but with the definition of the mad as totally alien. In his view, Pinel and Tuke widened the gap. Their achievement was only to develop more efficient ways to tame the mad, making it easier not to listen to them.

According to Foucault, Tuke and Pinel's guiding principle was conformity. If they struck down the chains of the mad, it was only to induce them to conform. For example, Pinel described an inmate who, believing himself the son of God, kept to himself addressing others only by imprecations. Pinel chose him as one of the first to be liberated. After freeing him from the chains with which he had been shackled for twelve years, Pinel instituted a policy of silence towards him. Slowly, Pinel reports, this messiah gave up his delusions and joined human society. This treatment epitomizes in Foucault's eyes the policy of non-dialogue. The wall of silence was Pinel's disqualifying response to the mad man's vociferations.[2]

Another example of non-dialogue is the pedagogic use of the faucet. In this treatment, an inmate's crazy talk was followed by a powerful stream of cold water upon the head. This treatment was repeated until the culprit gave up his deluded ideas. In Pinel's words: "Care [was] taken to avoid the hard tone and the shocking terms that would cause rebellion; on the contrary, the madman [was] made to understand that it [was] for his sake and reluctantly that we resort[ed] to such violent measures; sometimes we add[ed] a joke, taking care not to go too far with it" (Foucault 1965/1988, pp. 266–267).

It was Pinel who introduced the physician into the asylum as its ruling figure. Not however, for any special knowledge of his. On the contrary, Pinel stressed how useless medical knowledge was in dealing with the mad. However, the physician was the appropriate figure of authority, because of his emblematic

2. Here, we must confess, we find it hard to sympathize with Foucault's critique. It still seems better not to be talked to without chains then not to be talked to in chains.

status in society. The lord of the asylum owed his position not to his science, but to his standing as a pillar of the community. Thus was psychiatry born! Not because the mad person was viewed as falling into the province of the doctor's knowledge, but because the doctor signified authority without brute force! This is one of Foucault's best-known themes: the underside of knowledge is a power relation. It is also the goal of Foucault's genealogy: our anchoring notions about science, medicine, and madness are shown to have developed so arbitrarily that we are set epistemologically adrift, not unlike his Ship of Fools.

Gregory Bateson

If we were to choose the leading idea in Bateson's horn of plenty, we would signal his attitude to essentialist (or substantial) explanations. Like Molière's "Le Malade Imaginaire," we say that opium puts people to sleep because it possesses a *virtus dormitiva* (dormitive principle). The social sciences go even beyond Molière. They reify the sleeping disturbance itself, by attributing it to another essence, an *adormitosis*, which the opium palliates. Bateson's work might be viewed as an attempt to provide alternative explanations, replacing substances by patterns, relations, and messages. Mental illnesses are, of course, typical examples of putative substances that should be redescribed in these non-essentialist terms (Bateson 1972).

Consider a phenomenon such as aggression. In an essentialist frame of mind, we might search for the origins of this instinct or drive in the individual or species, trace its etiology and look for drugs to influence it. The whole enterprise, however, might have been falsely based on the assumption that there is a real entity, aggression, to be examined. Compare a wolf's aggression toward rival wolves and prey. The first takes place in a symmetrical context: the wolf's emission of dominance signs is enhanced by similar behavior in the antagonist. When one of the wolves' threatening or attacking moves are met by complementary moves of submission by the other, the aggression abates. Not so, however, when the wolf attacks a lamb. The lamb's submissive crouching would not reduce the wolf's aggression by a jot. From the point of view of the wolf, both kinds of aggression might have nothing in common. In Bateson's view, it makes more sense to look for similarities between various symmetrical (or complementary) patterns of interaction (aggressive or not) than between different manifestations of a reified drive, such as aggression. In other words, patterns are more interesting than entities. Following this principle, Bateson examined complementary and symmetrical patterns in the workings of society, the complexities of emotional expression, the vagaries of national character, and the dealings of the alcoholic with the bottle. In comparing these patterns, he taught us to focus on the nonsubstantial dance, rather than on the substantial dancers.

To return to the wolves. How does a wolf know that the other is emitting a real threat? Is exposure of the fangs, for instance, biologically wired to trigger defense or flight reactions (an essentialist hypothesis that postulates a defensive or escape drive activated by set stimuli)? Highly similar signals, however, are emitted when wolves only play at fighting. How do they know the difference? Bateson argues that in each case two kinds of message are relayed: the message "I have fangs to bite," and the message, "This is play" (or, "This is serious"). The second message qualifies the first. It is a *metamessage* that is, a message of higher logical order. Humans (as well as wolves) must learn to emit and identify these qualifying signals or pay the price for their ineptness. People who do not know when to take things seriously or playfully are exhibiting a metacommunicational failure. Some of these failures are essentialistically attributed to mental diseases, such as schizophrenia.

Bateson tells of a mental patient's mother whose home was kept exceedingly orderly and neat. Bateson gave her a bunch of gladioluses, saying he had wanted to give her something both beautiful and untidy. She replied, "Those are not untidy flowers. As each one withers you can snip it off" (Bateson 1972, pp. 198–199). Bateson felt that he too had been sort of snipped off, in having his remark demoted to the status of an apology. The woman had taken up his message, reclassified it as an apology and reacted to the reclassified message. The new message put her in a superior forgiving position. This kind of gambit was hypothesized by Bateson and his co-workers to characterize schizophrenic communication. This is the famous *double-bind hypothesis* (Bateson et al. 1956). The influence of the hypothesis extends far beyond its (less and less accepted) explanation of schizophrenia. It has played a vital role in the decline of psychopathological realism by shifting the focus from the individual's illness to the system's communication patterns.

MEMORY AND REALISM

Psychotherapy is popularly regarded as being based on the retrieval of submerged memories. This view is not wholly unjustified. Even today when psychotherapy is much more focused on the present, exploration of early history still plays a major role. A case presentation with no excursion into the client's early childhood would probably be viewed as deficient. The belief that the solution to the therapeutic puzzle lies hidden in the past is alive and kicking in the profession. Thus, whenever we stumble on a convincing reconstruction, particularly if accompanied by the emergence of vivid details and the live breath of renascent feelings, the meshes of skepticism are scattered. Indeed, to witness an outburst of spontaneous abreaction is a moving experience. The therapist who remains untouched, hiding behind a web of doubt in the face of relived pain, will often be suspected of lack of sympathy or of a crippling incapacity to believe.

Most people believe that everything we experience is permanently stored in the mind and that with the help of special techniques such as hypnosis, even the most inaccessible details can be recovered. Loftus and Loftus (1980) made a survey comparing endorsement of this proposition with an opposite one that states that many details are permanently lost from memory. Sixty-nine percent of non-psychologists expressed their belief in the first statement. Among psychologists, the rate of endorsement was 84 percent! The reasons adduced in favor of this belief ranged from the anecdotal recall of amazing details to reports attesting to the efficacy of hypnosis or psychoanalysis in the recovery of long-forgotten events. Special importance was attributed by psychologists to the findings of Penfield (1969) on the evocation of flashback memories by means of stimulation of the brain's temporal lobes. Penfield's patients did not merely remember; rather they seemed to fully reexperience the past. For example, if an evoked memory strip involved music, the patient could hum in time to it and report what instruments were being played. What would the skeptics say to that?

Eyewitness Memory

Elizabeth Loftus

Memories don't just fade, as the old saying would have us believe; they also grow (Loftus and Ketcham 1991, p. 20). Distortion may occur at any stage of memory processing, from acquisition, through retention, to retrieval. Loftus (1979) reviewed some of the classic studies on the inevitable distortions due to wishes, norms, and feelings, that occur at the stage of memory acquisition. She mentioned, for example: Allport and Postman's (1947) study showing that when a number of people are asked to relay serially what they saw in a visual stimulus involving a black man wearing a suit talking with a policeman who holds a razor, after a few relays, the razor passes from the hand of the policeman to that of the black man, the suit turns into jeans, and the conversation becomes a threat on the part of the black man. Loftus also described Bruner and Postman's (1949) study showing that subjects who are presented tachistoscopically with incongruent cards (for instance, a red ace of spades), contaminate their perception with their expectations, reporting that the spades were rusty black, or that it didn't even look like a card. Loftus also includes Hastorf and Cantrill's (1954) hilarious study of the fans of two football teams who watched the same game but saw two completely different ones.

These distortions at the stage of acquisition are compounded by additional distortions at the stage of retention. Memories are not simply retained (or gradually lost) but are continuously modified by ongoing mental activity. Thus, if subjects witness a video of a minor traffic accident and are later asked a suggestive question like, "How fast were the cars going when they *smashed* into each other?" their description of the accident will be modified to accommodate the suggestion. For instance, they may report on splintered glass where there wasn't any. Moreover, if the same subjects are later re-exposed to the original video, as well as to another showing splintered glass, they will tend to say that the one with splintered glass was the original one (Loftus 1979). In addition, Loftus reports that the original memory seems to be all but unrecoverable. Subjects were offered pecuniary incentives, given the chance of a second guess, exposed to counter-suggestive influences, but to no avail: the original memory traces seemed to have been permanently modified by the new ones.

The circumstances of the retrieval stage also affect memory reports. Trying to retrieve information in a setting different from the one where the acquisition took place will not only lead to lower accuracy rates, but will often give rise to a mixed recall built out of both sets of circumstances. A similar distortion will follow biased questions. Asking, for instance, "How short was the basketball player?" will bring different estimates of height than asking "How tall was the basketball player?" Asking, "Do you get headaches frequently, and if so, how often?" brings out estimates three times as large as asking, "Do you get headaches occasionally, and if so, how often?" (Loftus 1979). The very act of reporting one's memories is another source of distortion. After being exposed to the frequency version of the headaches question, subjects' reports of headaches tend to freeze around the higher estimate. Putting memories into words is no neutral act of translation: words seem to change the inner images, crystalizing them in a new form. With each new verbalization, people's confidence in the veracity of retrieved memories grows. Each time a witness is asked to re-identify a suspect, her confidence grows, independent of the truth of the identification.

This power of words over images is beautifully shown in the following report of an early memory by Jean Piaget:

> I was sitting in my pram, which my nurse was pushing in the Champs Elysées, when a man tried to kidnap me. I was held in by the strap fastened round me while my nurse bravely tried to stand between me and the thief. She received various scratches, and I can still see vaguely those on her face. Then a crowd gathered, a policeman with a short cloak and a white baton came up, and the man took to his heels. I can still see the whole scene, and can even place it near the tube station. When I was about fifteen, my parents received

> a letter from my former nurse saying that she had been converted to the Salvation Army. She wanted to confess her past faults, and in particular to return the watch she had been given as a reward on this occasion. She had made up the whole story, faking the scratches. I, therefore, must have heard, as a child, the account of this story, which my parents believed, and projected it into the past in the form of a visual memory [1962, pp. 187–188].

But what of Penfield's demonstration (1969) of the effects of electrical stimulation of the brain? A close look at the data reveals that flashback memories were aroused only in a small proportion of subjects (about 3 percent). The other 97 percent seemed to be refractory even to the most persistent electrical digging. As for the 3 percent, how could we be assured that a strip of the past was really made present? In no case was the evidence independently corroborated (nor could it be, for the memories were usually of routine events). Perhaps Penfield's patients were imagining or hallucinating. Perhaps electrical stimulation aroused in them a state of high suggestibility, in which inner events are experienced with great vividness. Perhaps these 3 percent were highly suggestible to begin with. None of these questions has been dealt with. The neurological evidence for the rocklike permanence of memory traces seems to crumble at the touch.

Loftus (1979) has brought to the judicial trials in which she has given depositions a dose of skepticism that went against the prevailing tendency of juries to take the reliability of memory (particularly, the memory of victims) for granted. In this role, she has also earned considerable hatred. Mothers whose daughters had been raped and wives of murdered husbands have more than once flung their bitter allegations at the protector of the wicked. Loftus has also aroused indignation on the part of clinicians for daring to question the dependability of their clients' recall of early traumatic experiences. Skepticism has never been popular with psychotherapists. It is therefore highly significant that at the very heart of psychoanalysis, the school that more than any other could lay claim to a special relationship with the distant past, a skeptical trend concerning memory should have developed.

Memory in Psychoanalysis

Freud often compared psychoanalysis to archaeology. At times he would even claim that the psychoanalyst has clear advantages over the archaeologist, because the submerged mental contents are kept undamaged in the unconscious, whereas only fragments of the physical remains of previous eras are preserved (Freud 1937/1976). In classical psychoanalysis, the past is deemed to be connected to the present by a straight causal chain. Symptoms are the outcome of early events that must be recovered if cure is to occur. The psychoanalytic method, viewed as fully neutral and objective, should allow for the surfacing of the submerged material without affecting its nature. The end result of a successful psychoanalysis must, therefore, be an exact and compelling reconstruction of the client's early life.

Roy Schafer

Schafer (1976, 1983) based his critique of this credo on the idea of the *hermeneutic circle*. First proposed by Schleiermacher (Woolfolk et al. 1988), the hermeneutic circle is a conceptualization of knowledge as inescapably contextual: a fact, or any putative unit of knowledge, does not stand on its own, but can only be apprehended through the very context it helps to define. Words have meaning in and by the sentence they constitute and observations can be understood only through the theories they uphold. Memories, likewise, are never free from context, but are summoned up and interpreted in terms of a present frame of mind. In therapy, memories are influenced also by the give-and-take with the analyst, whose theories are constituted by and constitutive of this self-same memory material. Thus, no aboriginal body of objective evidence can ever be reached.

Constrained by the hermeneutic circle, memory must involve reconstruction. Events cannot be recalled without being redescribed, reinterpreted and reassessed through a new context or leading narrative. Thus, our childhood memories, rather than reproductions of the world we saw as children, are complex translations into the adult mind of what we believe to have happened; we even witness ourselves in the third person in a scene we could never have experienced (redescription). Moreover, we cannot think of childhood events without overlaying them with adult meanings (reinterpretation). Finally, the values are invariably changed: old trivia are remembered as invaluable while major catastrophes turn ludicrous (reassessment). Ideally, we should be able to separate the elaboration of the present from the raw data of the past. Schafer, however, is skeptical. There are simply no raw data to be had.

Memory is thus circular: the past is used to help understand the present and vice-versa, with both being changed in the process. This perspective changes our conception of basic psychoanalytic processes. Transference, for instance, was once viewed as a road to the hidden past. Schafer argues, however, that far from working as a time machine, transference should be regarded as doing just the opposite. Particular memories are construed so as to fit the developments in the analytic relationship. Transference is thus stood on its head! In Schafer's description, the only history of which the therapist may feel reasonably secure is the history of the therapy.

Donald Spence

Schafer's critique appeared at about the same time as Donald Spence's (1982) analysis of historical truth and narrative truth in psychoanalysis. Narrative truth refers to the feeling that all the elements of an account hang together, to the sense of inevitability in a well-constructed mystery tale, and to the compelling power of a given solution that makes us say that it *must* be so. Its major criteria are coherence, comprehensiveness, and parsimony. Thus, an elegant interpretation, a detailed reconstruction of past events, a well-rounded case history, may be said to possess narrative truth. According to Freud, however, the goodness of fit between the many parts of the analytic account bear witness to the historical truth of the reconstruction. The interpretation could not work were it not for the presence of such historical truth. The logically compelling power of the reconstruction shows that things did indeed happen so. Psychoanalytic theory rests on this foundation: the findings of analysis must reflect the true course of development.

In the Freudian view, the guarantor of psychoanalytic reliability is the objectivity and neutrality of the psychoanalytic method. The basic data of analysis are the client's free-floating associations. The client is instructed to report everything that comes to mind, without selection, like a traveler in a train observing the landscape (Freud 1913/1976). The therapist's counterpart to the client's neutral free-association is the attitude of evenly hovering attention, a passive-receptive frame of mind that precludes any theoretical biasing of the material. The meeting of these two neutral attitudes makes for the validity of psychoanalytic data.

Spence argues that client and therapist labor under a constant pressure towards meaning that makes free-floating association and evenly hovering attention all but impossible. In communicating, we must order, divide, and freeze into words a mental stream that is naturally disorderly, fused, and fleeting. Trying to capture in words the everchanging multitude of this mental stream is, in William James's unforgettable metaphor, like "trying to cut a thought in two to look at its section [or] . . . seize a spinning top to catch its motion" (James 1890/1950, p. 244). The very process of choosing words to translate inner experience is agonizingly slow, compared with the speed of the inner flow. Indeed, if the client really tried to say all that came to mind, she would be nothing like a serene traveler in a train, but rather like a crazy runner, hopelessly chasing after the quickly receding images.

However felicitous the client's words in capturing some of the stream of consciousness's shifting iridescence, a further problem remains: the emitted associations must make sense to the therapist. To this end, the client must supply context. If, for instance, a client reports on events connected with his boss, and the boss had in the past been involved with the client's wife, an explanatory digression will have to be made, thus changing the original direction of the flow. Alternatively, if the client decides not to supply the needed context (following the basic rule of free-association to the letter), his associations will probably become a solipsistic word torrent. Therefore, either the associations are not free (and the data of psychoanalysis are not neutral) or the analyst cannot hope to comprehend them.

Indeed, if the therapist is faced with a loosely connected stream of words, she cannot respond with evenly hovering attention. The more free the associations, the more is the therapist compelled to supply her own context (usually created by theoretical presuppositions) to make sense of the material. Evenly hovering attention is thus possible only when the client supplies enough context to make understanding possible, that is, when he is not freely associating!

Without neutral data, Spence argues, psychoanalysis loses its grounding on a dependable personal history. The stories that are built in analysis are inevitably reconstructions, heavily influenced by the beliefs and interests of the participants. Although for the client the process of therapy may remain the same, the scientific status of psychoanalytic theory and the objective reality of what it purports to describe suffer badly from Spence's critique.

Hypnotic Memory

One of the major reasons adduced by professionals for their belief in the permanence of memory was their acquaintance, direct or indirect, with the hypnotic recovery of long-forgotten events (Loftus and Loftus 1980). Hypnotic memory carries conviction through its sensory and emotional richness, compared with which the carpings of critical reasoning seem pale indeed. The best answer to skeptics is often simply an invitation for anyone to come and see.

Perhaps even more convincing are some well-documented miracles of hypnotic retrieval. The most famous of all may be the Chowchilla kidnapping case, in which one of the victims reconstructed under hypnosis the license plate number of the kidnappers' van, leading to their eventual capture (Kroger and Douce 1979). Such examples all but pull the carpet from under the critics' feet. Something must be deeply wrong with the skeptics' contentions if such superhuman feats of memory are at all possible.

In the course of the last twenty years, however, dozens of laboratory and field investigations of hypnotic memory have given rise to a different picture. In one variety of study, subjects are exposed to the material to be remembered (a videotape, a series of slides, or an apparently unplanned event) and at a later stage are asked to recall or recognize the original data with or without hypnosis. The time lapse between the original event and the attempted reconstruction ranges from a few days to many months. The verdict of research after a long series of such studies is quite unanimous: hypnotic memory is not better (it actually tends to be worse) then nonhypnotic memory (Orne et al. 1991). Furthermore, subjects who recall under hypnosis are much more confident about their own accuracy, even when they are wrong (Dinges et al. 1987, Whitehouse et al. 1987)! To make matters worse, the hypnotic subjects are also clearly more amenable to influence by leading questions (Putnam 1979). These findings show that hypnotic memory can be not only inaccurate, but also misleading: subjects exude a degree of confidence that their actual performance betrays.

The hypnotic phenomenon of age regression has also been brought under the critical scrutiny of research. The two central questions investigated were: whether the memories recovered while a subject is age regressed are more reliable than otherwise; and whether age-regressed subjects manifest behavior and mental states typical of the ages to which they are regressed. The verdict of research on both questions is negative. When subjects are asked under hypnosis to recall verifiable items, such as the day of the week of past birthdays or the names of former teachers and schoolmates, they do no better than subjects not under hypnosis (Perry et al. 1991). As for their behavior and mental state, it shows no similarity to children of the same age to which they are regressed (Nash 1987). In one of the few studies that upheld the veracity of age regression (Reiff and Scheerer 1959), adult subjects were regressed to the age of 4 and asked to play in a sandbox. When their hands were covered with sand, they were given a lollipop with the candy side toward them. They invariably picked the lollipop by the candy side without bothering about their dirty hands. Quite a demonstration that they felt and behaved like small children! In a recent replication, a control group of actual 4-year olds was used: they all picked the lollipop by the stick (see also O'Connell et al. 1970)!

Real life hypnosis seems to occasion mistakes and distortions no less blatant than laboratory hypnosis. The case of *State v. Mack* (1980) in Minnesota showed hypnotic confabulation at work in a way that led to that state's supreme court ruling that witnesses could not testify about their hypnotically elicited reminiscences in court—a ruling which was followed by most other states in ensuing years (Perry et al. 1991). The case dealt with a woman who started bleeding after having had sexual intercourse in a motel. She went to a hospital and the examining physician volunteered that she had probably been injured by a hard instrument. This remark made her phone the police. Since she had no memories of assault, she was offered hypnosis as a memory aid. Under hypnosis she remembered that her partner had stabbed her repeatedly in the vagina with a knife. The court, however, rejected her testimony, for it failed the test of a serious medical examination (she had only one internal vaginal lesion consistent with her gynecological history with no injury to the external labia).[3]

---

3. One of the most horrifying and best documented cases of judicial errors due to hypnotic phenomena is reported by Ofshe (1992).

The significance of these findings for psychotherapy is far-reaching: besides casting doubt on the permanence of memories, they also point to circumstances that may vitiate the client's reports. Indeed, psychotherapy shares many features with hypnosis, such as the encouragement of a passive, free-floating and dream-like state of mind. If we add to this the common belief of clients that the therapist or hypnotist knows more about them than they do, we are confronted with a situation that can be highly conducive to believed imaginings (Sarbin and Coe 1972).

THE DECLINING REALITY OF THE SELF

At the very center of realist beliefs in psychotherapy lies the self. Unitary, enduring, and private, it is the core of individuality. It may be hidden, disguised, or obscured. It is often neglected and warped in the course of development. Still, it can be reached and by patient work restored. Indeed, the restoration of the self is one of the highest hopes of psychotherapy. This realist view, however appealing, has been trenchantly criticized and an alternative perspective on the self as a many sided narrative has been proposed. The development of this new perspective has been chronicled in detail by two of its major proponents, Bruner (1990) and Gergen (1991).

Jerome Bruner

The initial step away from a realistic view of the self, according to Bruner, was the understanding that it cannot be directly perceived. We are not endowed with organs or abilities to apprehend it directly. We must therefore construe a *concept* of the self. A construed self is definitely less palpable than a perceived one. Moreover, once the self had been conceived of as construed, interest became focused on the processes (particularly interpersonal ones) that might affect the construal.

Social psychologists, for instance, turned out many intriguing observations on the self-concept. For instance: (1.) subjects interviewed by someone instructed to assess their degree of introversion viewed themselves as more introverted than those who were interviewed by someone instructed to assess their degree of extroversion (Snyder 1984); (2.) subjects asked to play a particular role in a group changed their self-image in a manner congruent with the role (Gergen and Taylor 1969); and (3.) subjects who interacted with others defined as powerful viewed themselves as diminished, relative to subjects who interacted with others defined as lacking in power (Morse and Gergen 1970). Surprisingly, the impact of these context-manipulated self-descriptions seemed to last well beyond the time of the experiments (Fazio et al. 1981).

A further solvent to the reality of the self was added by the advent of narrative concepts. Almost all approaches in social, individual, and clinical psychology were deeply affected by the expanding narrative perspective (e.g., Bruner 1986, Sarbin 1986, White and Epston 1990). Theoreticians seemed entranced by the view that one's versions of self keep changing, just as one's possible futures and pasts. We can only *be* by *narrating* ourselves to others, who are equally narratively defined (Schafer 1982). The self is a tale told to a tale.

An eery feeling creeps in. Is this all we are? Has not the process of dereification gone a bit too far? Are our identities no more substantial than mouthfuls of air or the turns of a story? Bruner has a ready answer: narratives are no mere flights of fancy but the means by which we create order and stability out of chaos. Drawing from his lifelong involvement and acquaintance with developmental research, Bruner argues that from earliest childhood we organize our experience narratively, even before we are possessed of words with which to dress our storied constructs. Far from depending on language, our inborn narrative tendency provides the push that determines the order and manner of language acquisition. This ubiquity of narrative is shown, for instance, by children's early tendency to focus on storylike occurrences in the environment, the abundance of story episodes in spontaneous maternal speech[4], and the universal organization of language in terms of agent–action–object. At the age of 4, children are already equipped not only with the ability to understand stories, but with a strong tendency to set them into canonical forms. Thus, telling a child a story that violates expected forms (such as a story of a birthday girl who was unhappy, or of a birthday boy who poured water on the candles) leads to ten times as many elaborations by the child as telling a

4. An average count of 8.5 narratives per hour was reported as characteristic of mothers in a blue-collar neighborhood in Baltimore (Miller, 1982).

story that follows expected forms (Bruner 1990). The elaborations are almost invariably attempts to bring the story into line or to explain the deviations. This storying ability, furthermore, is not only a key to the child's understanding of the environment, but also one of her major social tools. Stories are used very early to flatter, to blame, and to gain sympathy or forgiveness.

Bruner's revealing disquisition on the role of narratives in the organization of experience is a Kantian revolution of sorts. Just as Kant attempted to show that the world was fixed and lawful, not by nature, but because our mental apparatus makes it so, Bruner argues that narratives are not mere implements by which we describe a pre-existing orderly reality, but the very tools by which reality is ordered. Therefore it is not disparaging to say that the self is a tale. It is merely putting order back where it belongs.

Kenneth Gergen

In the story of the self as told by Gergen, the emphasis shifts from the cognitive to the sociocultural arena. For as long as our social reality was reasonably uniform and stable, our sense of self was stable, too. The enormous changes brought about by communicational technologies, however, have created a world in which we are constantly bombarded with new models and new mores. Unceasing invitations for new and strange experiences, roles, and perspectives arrive from everywhere. Gergen (1991) coined the term *multiphrenia* for this condition.

One might argue, perhaps, that although cultural messages define the specific contents of our experience, they do not determine the self's very essence. The self is the self under a Christian, a totalitarian, or a pop-cultural dispensation. The contents may vary, but not the personal substratum. But is it so? Gergen bids us consider the Balinese, who are wont to view individuals only as representatives of general social categories. Individuality is so de-emphasized that loving or hating someone on the basis of his personal characteristics makes little sense. People are related to as parents, uncles, firstborns, or as members of a profession, clan, or social class. Names are given to define the person's place in the social matrix, changing as this place changes throughout the individual's life. In such a culture, what would be the meaning of an individualized self? How could one decide whether someone was behaving in a manner true to self or was merely wearing a social mask? This very question, so pertinent in our culture, is senseless to the Balinese.

Consider our brave new world. The age is one of mobility. Fewer and fewer people live their lives within a single community and many cross different cultural boundaries daily. Those with whom we share any of our social frames are often complete strangers to those who populate our other frames. This social disjunction allows us to adopt quite different and at times, opposite life styles, in different life areas. Many are hard-nosed workers by day and lotus-eaters by night. Urban anonymity guarantees the feasibility of such variegated self-projects. Add to this the infinite experiences brought to us by the media. We move from the apartments of the Queen of England, to a meal with the anthropophagi, to the hysterics of a rock concert all within three clicks of our remote control. Movie stars, writers, philosophers, players, and painters parade before us. If we happen to be sued by a spouse, attacked by a robber, or harassed by a maniac, the situation is not wholly new to us; we have been there, vicariously. Additionally, we are positively encouraged to experiment with different social mores by our very emphasis on cultural tolerance and interchange. Only bigoted fanatics will have no truck with the riches available in a multiethnic society.

There are other essentials of the self that can be had almost for the asking: body parts, hormone refills, mood pills. Even gender is no longer destiny. Within this whirligig, what can we do with Polonius's advice to Laertes: "To thine own self alone be true"?

The center does not hold and the one self explodes into a multiplicity of contexts. New terms are coined apace for our kaleidoscopic identities: *the protean self* (Lifton 1993), *the mutable self* (Zurcher 1977), *the pastiche personality* (Gergen 1991). Most amazingly, these are often presented in a favorable light, in contrast to the decided preference of an earlier generation for the solid, inner-directed over the fickle, outer-directed personality (Riesman 1950).

SCIENTIFIC PSYCHOTHERAPY

The strictly scientific status of psychotherapy is usually professed aloud, but questioned silently. The scientific affiliation is deemed vital for contrasting psychotherapy with alternative forms of mental healing that are less prestigious in our culture. The claim of psychotherapy to scientific status has rested on its reliance on research and on the dedication to truth inherent in its practice. In recent years, however, this reliance and dedication has become problematic. The profession seems to be caught in a quandary: standing either for or against a binding linkage with science involves one either in wishful thinking or irresponsibility.

The Hope of Research

Paradoxically, the verdict of research that contributed most to legitimize psychotherapy has also laid bare the precariousness of its scientific hopes. Research came into psychotherapy, first and foremost, to crown the winner among the competing approaches. Unbounded theoretical multiplicity could be accepted only as a temporary affliction, a childhood illness of the field. A scientific discipline can bear with a couple of competing theories temporarily fighting for supremacy (Kuhn 1962) but the permanent coexistence of dozens of mutually contradictory approaches would cast serious doubts on its status as a science. This, however, seems to be precisely the condition psychotherapy has to put up with, if we are to trust the results of outcome research. It seems that although psychotherapy in general has been shown to be helpful, no approach can claim decided superiority over others (Luborsky et al. 1975, Smith et al. 1980). This equivalence finding (nicknamed *The Dodo Bird Verdict*) has been replicated again and again, despite considerable evidence that the various therapeutic approaches really *are* different in practice (Stiles et al. 1986). What scientifically based advice could a professional then give to those who ask for a fitting therapy for their ills—that although each approach claims that all others are mistaken—actually all are equally good and true? Such advice would earn little respect for the profession.

Maybe the hope for the vindication of a single approach was simplistic to begin with. Indeed, sophisticated researchers have long given up this unitary goal in favor of a more refined one. The question for research should not simply be which approach is best? but rather *which* treatment, by *whom*, is most effective for *this* individual with *that* specific problem, and under *which* set of circumstances? (Paul 1967). Research should aim not at one winner but at a multidimensional matrix. For a while the matrix ideal became the guiding beacon of research. Thousands of studies were conducted (Omer and Dar 1992), attempting to connect between any two dimensions of the matrix. The results were disappointing: not a single cell of the matrix has been filled to the satisfaction of most investigators.

Apart from this chronic inconclusiveness, two further problems threaten to relegate the whole matrix paradigm to the realms of fantasy. First, the sheer magnitude of the task: ten varieties of treatments, therapists, clients, problems, and settings would yield a matrix of 100,000 cells (Stiles et al. 1986)! Second, the parameters that define the matrix refuse to stay put. Each season yields its harvest of new treatments, diagnoses, and therapist profiles, while older ones become rapidly dated. Who remembers today the difference between type A and type B therapists that seemed so pertinent as to merit dozens of studies just a while ago? The matrix project might perhaps be fea-

sible if we had a theoretical rationale for defining its dimensions (Beutler 1979). But what reason is there for supporting any specific theoretical rationale? No empirical matrix would be needed if matters could be solved by theoretical fiat to begin with.

A different tack is followed by the *common factors* approach to research: different treatments work similarly well because they share the factors that determine change (Frank 1961/1973). Therapists, however, need *differential* guidelines from research, not a generalized endorsement. The common factors approach may be a good way of doing research about psychotherapy but it hardly furthers a differentiated scientific practice. Indeed, the common factors approach tells therapists: it is not important what you do, as long as you do it with full conviction and establish a good relationship with the client within a socially endorsed framework. Little wonder that therapists are not overjoyed by this news.

If they only could, many therapists would perhaps choose to ignore the verdict of research. Health insurance policies, however, stipulate that only a therapy that adduces adequate research evidence in its favor should be reimbursable (Parloff 1982). Psychotherapy finds itself financially trapped in its own scientific net! Therapists must make use of the legitimization that comparative research affords them, even though it also legitimizes the therapeutic opposition! The equivalence findings of research are thus a boon to the pocket, but a blow to the soul. In spite of its financial significance, however, the standing of traditional research in psychotherapy seems to be losing ground. In the wake of influential attacks on the sacrosanctity of the scientific method as such (Feyerabend 1975, Kuhn 1962), trenchant critiques of ruling scientific procedures have surfaced also in psychology and psychotherapy (Gergen 1982, Manicas and Secord 1983, Polkinghorne 1983). Most of these are reformist in intent, but some gleefully claim that the downfall of our belief in an ultimately knowable reality has killed the sacred cow of research (Hoffman 1992).

The Therapist's Dedication to Truth

Psychotherapists have traditionally equated the therapeutic attitude with the scientist's dedication to truth. Cure was viewed as the natural consequence of the therapist's scientific attitude. Psychoanalysis worked through its very neutrality and objectivity, behavior therapy by transforming the clinic into a laboratory, and cognitive therapy by extending scientific rationality to life. Even the advocates of existentialist and humanist approaches were unwilling to sever the therapy-science connection. Laing (1959) attacked psychiatric objectification in the very name of a real science of persons. Similarly, for many Rogerians, only a thoroughly non-judgmental and non-directive therapy could embody the free spirit of science and allow personal truth to emerge unencumbered.

This precious identity between science and therapy has been deeply shaken. Total objectivity and neutrality have been shown to be pious positivist dreams. The supposed discovery of the forgotten past, the hidden mind, and the true self has been recast as the *construction* of a new reality, not necessarily less biased than the one that was dismissed. For many practitioners, dedication to truth stopped being an ideal. This process did not necessarily lower the therapist's self-image. Sometimes the opposite was true. Untrammeled by the shackles of objectivity, therapists could now become veritable demiurges of change. Therapy books soared, even in their titles: *Frogs into Princes, The Eagle, Practical Magic, My Voice Will Go With You.* Self-discipline became obsolete, and sliding from truth, not only condonable but enjoyable. One blithe clinician, an ex-rabbi, specialized in lofty Talmudic pseudoquotes for the benefit of his clients.

Misinformation became legitimized once the scientific attitude had been left behind: therapists no longer felt committed to their role as representatives of knowledge. This state of affairs, however, was not always (or even usually) communicated to clients. Practitioners still presented themselves to clients as the repositories of psychological wisdom. This is precisely the way of turning psychotherapy into downright quackery. Hopefully, truth-spurning will prove only to be a passing fringe affliction of the profession.

THE EPISTEMOLOGICAL QUANDARY

In the schools' era therapists had a clear sense of direction: their theory told them where they were heading and how their clients' problems had originated. Within each approach treatments were reasonably homogeneous and consistent. The therapeutic journey might be long, but therapists were equipped with map and compass to steer their course. The criteria for judging treatment constructs were clear: a therapeutic move was right if it fit with the truths and mores of the approach one belonged to. There was no confusion about what counted as positive outcome. Psychoanalysts were not bothered by manifest behavior nor were behaviorists by insight. Today, these certainties have been undermined and the modern practitioner faces a perplexing professional reality.

Some gloried in the downfall of absolute certainties. The iconoclastic glee and the conceptual orgy that engendered slogans such as: "Anything goes!" "Let the signifiers frolic!" and "Go piss against the wind!" cannot, however, have any more hold than beer foam spilt on a table. Most psychotherapists continued all the while searching for values to fill the void, and many of those who began by experiencing the libertarian exhilaration have in the meantime sobered up. However, the way back to the lost Eden of total beliefs seemed blocked. A search was therefore launched for multiple dialogues (Saltzman and Norcross 1990), convergent themes (Goldfried 1982), and pluralist criteria (Strenger and Omer 1992). The brightest dream (or bleakest nightmare) was perhaps that of a wall-to-wall harmonious integration that would restore a sense of peace and rest to the torn field. As most surmise, this is not to be. The general understanding that pluralism and relativism are probably here to stay shows itself in the very name that searchers for dialogue and convergence have given to their fellowship: The Society for *Exploration* of Psychotherapy Integration.

Indeed, it seems that our professional truths will have to remain provisional and consensual. We will go on *exploring* the ways for achieving an ever more satisfactory integration and consensus. The width of the consensus is of course crucial in a world such as ours, where a plurality of views obtains. We would hope for our beliefs to achieve the most varied consensual endorsement. The role given to scientific practice, in this account, is of course a different one than in the positivist era. Science and research are no longer the final arbiters of absolute truth, but simply very well-tried procedures for multiple debate and consensual validation. But that precisely is their strength. We might say, with no trepidation, that the mores embodied in scientific practice provide us with one of the most widely accepted and well-tried procedures for a pluralist exchange of ideas. For this reason, we believe that research plays a vital role even under a pluralist dispensation. It is, no less than before, one of the most powerful antidotes against the anarchy of "anything goes."

The ideals of honesty and consensual validation that have guided scientific practice throughout the ages are also highly relevant, in our view, to the field of therapeutic narrative. We would certainly reject as downright dishonest therapeutic narratives to which the therapist did not himself subscribe. We would also be highly suspicious of therapeutic narratives that proved acceptable only to a narrow coterie of like-minded practitioners. We would have our narratives be acceptable not only to the therapist and the client, but also to others such as family members, different therapists, institutional representatives, and academics (Strenger and Omer 1992). We would then achieve a higher degree of consensual validation. Our approach to narrative thus turns out to be not absolutely different from our approach to science. The methods of exposition and persuasion may vary, but both, the scientific and the narrative pursuits, aim at establishing conviction with the widest and most varied audiences. We would like to go on widening the circle of discussion and consensus by having our readers participate.[5]

5. We would be glad to receive any response to our narrative principles and examples. Our addresses for correspondence are: Haim Omer, Department of Psychology, Tel-Aviv University, Ramat-Aviv, 69978, Israel; Nahi Alon, 9 Bat-Yam Street, Jaffa, Israel.

REFERENCES

Abrams, M. H. (1971). *Natural Supernaturalism.* New York: Norton.

Adams, D. (1982). *The Restaurant at the End of the Universe.* London: Pan Books.

Alexander, F. and French, T. M. (1946). *Psychoanalytic Therapy: Principles and Applications.* New York: Ronald Press.

Allport, G. W. and Postman, L. J. (1947). *The Psychology of Rumor.* New York: Henry Holt.

Alon, N. (1985). An Ericksonian approach to the treatment of chronic posttraumatic patients. In *Ericksonian Psychotherapy, vol. II,* ed. J.K. Zeig. New York: Brunner/Mazel.

Andersen, T. (1987). The reflecting team: dialogue and meta-dialogue in clinical work. *Family Process,* 26, 415–428.

Anderson, H. and Goolishian, H. A. (1988). Human systems as linguistic systems: preliminary and evolving ideas about the implications for clinical theory. *Family Process*, 27, 371–393.

Auerbach, E. (1953). Odysseus' scar. In *Mimesis: The Representation of Reality in Western Literature,* ed. E. Auerbach. Princeton, NJ: Princeton University Press.

Baier, K. (1981). The meaning of life. In *The Meaning of Life,* ed. E. D. Klemke. Oxford: Oxford University Press.

Bakhtin, M. (1984). *Rabelais and His World.* Bloomington: Indiana University Press.

Bandura, A. (1969). *Principles of Behavior Modification*. New York: Holt, Rinehart & Winston.

Bandura, A., and Walters, R. H. (1959). *Adolescent Aggression*. New York: Ronald Press.

Bateson, G. (1972). *Steps to an Ecology of Mind.* New York: Ballantine.

Bateson, G., Jackson, D. D., Haley, J., and Weakland, J. H. (1956). Towards a theory of schizophrenia. *Behavioral Science* 1: 251–264.

Beutler, L. E. (1979). Toward specific psychological therapies for specific conditions. *Journal of Consulting and Clinical Psychology* 47: 882–897.

Bjornson, R. (1977). *The Picaresque Hero in European Fiction.* Madison, WI: University of Wisconsin Press.

Boscolo, L., Cecchin, G., Hoffman, L. and Penn, P. (1987). *Milan Systemic Family Therapy.* New York: Basic Books.

Breuer, J., and Freud, S. (1893/1955). Studies in hysteria. *Standard Edition* 1.

Bruner, J. (1986). *Actual Minds, Possible Worlds.* Cambridge, MA: Harvard University Press.

____ (1990). *Acts of Meaning.* Cambridge, MA: Harvard University Press.

Bruner, J. S., and Postman, L. (1949). On the perception of incongruity: a paradigm. *Journal of Personality* 18: 206–223.